James S. [?]
from the author

Karl H. Eschman

Nov. 24, 1945

CHANGING FORMS IN MODERN MUSIC

BY

KARL ESCHMAN

Jessie King Wiltsee Professor of Music
Denison University

E. C. SCHIRMER MUSIC COMPANY
BOSTON, MASSACHUSETTS

16844 83

CONTENTS

		PAGE
	PREFACE. IN DEFENSE OF THE SUBJECT	vii
I.	WHAT HAS HAPPENED TO MUSIC?	1
II.	ÆSTHETICS OF A CHANGING STANDARD	13
III.	THE MUSICAL SENTENCE AND ITS HARMONIC PUNCTUATION	26
IV.	PHRASE DETERMINATION IN MELODIC INFLECTION	50
V.	THE MEASURE OF THE RHYTHM	62
VI.	NEW SYSTEMS OF DIFFERENTIATED MATERIALS	81
VII.	THE MODERN VARIATION PRINCIPLE	111
VIII.	MODERN PRIMARY FORMS AND THEIR HYBRIDS	130
IX.	THE MODERN SONATA	140
X.	THE FUGUE IN MODERN MUSIC	150
XI.	IN CONCLUSION	159
	APPENDIX	165

ACKNOWLEDGMENTS

The author gratefully acknowledges the kindness of the publishers or their American representatives who have given permission to reproduce musical examples from copyrighted works. The companies and the works from which illustrations are drawn are as follows:

To **Am-Rus Music Corporation**, New York, for SHOSTAKOVICH'S *Preludes*.

To **Arrow Music Press, Inc.**, New York, for AARON COPLAND'S *Piano Variations*.

To **Associated Music Publishers, Inc.**, New York, for HÁBA'S *Second Quarter-tone Quartet*, and *Fantasie for Violin Solo*, Opus 9a; HAUER'S *Fantasie*, Opus 37; JARNACH'S *Allegretto;* KRENEK'S *Toccata and Chaconne*, Opus 13; SATIE'S *Cinq Grimaces;* SCHOENBERG'S *Drei Klavierstücke*, Opus 11; *Sechs Kleine Stücke*, Opus 19, and *Suite*, Opus 25; SLAVENSKI'S *Albanischer Gesang*, and WEBERN'S *Morgenlied*.

To **Boosey and Hawkes, Ltd.**, London, and **Boosey and Hawkes, Inc.**, New York agents, for BÉLA BARTÓK'S *Fourth String Quartet*, *Piano Suite, Für Kinder*, and *Piano Sonata*, and RICHARD STRAUSS' *Salome*.

To **Durand & Cie**, France, and **Elkan-Vogel Co., Inc.**, Philadelphia, for DALCROZE'S *50 Études Miniatures*, and HONEGGER'S *First Sonata for Violin and Piano*.

To **Carl Fischer, Inc.**, New York, for LEO ORNSTEIN'S *Poems of 1917*.

To **G. Schirmer, Inc.**, New York, for WALLINGFORD RIEGGER'S *Blue Voyage*.

ACKNOWLEDGMENTS

In addition, the author wishes to express his deep appreciation:

To BÉLA BARTÓK and GUSTAVE REESE, Associate Editor of the *Musical Quarterly,* for the *Hungarian Folk-Song* — quoted on page 114.

To DARIUS MILHAUD, for permission to use his *Piano Sonata* (1917).

To ARTUR SCHNABEL, for the quotation from his *Sonata for Solo Violin.*

To the **Music Teachers' National Association,** for permission to use material from various articles prepared by the author for that Association.

To the **Denison Research Foundation,** for a grant in aid of publication.

To ERNEST C. SCHIRMER, for his interest and encouragement, and to HENRY CLOUGH-LEIGHTER, for his untiring editorial assistance.

To ERWIN STEIN, for permission to quote the outline of the forms in ALBAN BERG'S Opera: *Wozzeck*, and, more especially, for his many kindnesses in Vienna. And finally, to the members of the author's family, who have helped in so many ways during the preparation of this book.

PREFACE

The last fifty years have witnessed important changes in the art of music. Since the death of Wagner, if we may accept that as a convenient date, the freedom in tonal relationships which he advanced has been still further enlarged until it is difficult to discover in some modern music any centripetal attraction whatever. In this freedom the new harmony has contributed interesting additions to the musical vocabulary, and these have received more attention up to the present than the related problems of rhetoric. The need of articulation and the demand for cogency in the music — in short, all the problems of form — remain, although the methods of musical punctuation have changed. It is in the hope of contributing something to the understanding of the newer musical rhetoric, that this book has been written.

A technical analysis always meets with some objections. If there is special need for a defense of that branch of Theory of music which includes the analysis of form, this may be due to the fact that the present age is not especially analytical in temperament. Its art is restive under any restrictions other than those which come from within the individual, who is urged to throw off all restraint in the expression of his idiosyncrasies. We cannot take for granted complete sympathy with the methods of analysis used in the past, nor even any general agreement as to the need for detailed analysis at all.

Much, however, depends upon the methods used and the spirit in which analysis is undertaken. If we attempt to fit new compositions to the old Procrustean beds, there is just ground for criticism. If, on the other hand, we realize that in art, as in biology, no two organisms are the same, then we will seek to understand them as individuals of species which are still evolving.

It is true that the composer is not thinking primarily of analyses. His work is synthetic and his sense of form, more or less intuitive, a very important element in his natural genius. So it is, to some extent, on down the line: in performers, critics, and students, as well as in the individuals who make up our concert audiences. There are those who say that if a man does not have this sense of form after repeated rehearsals or re-hearings of a work, that ends the matter. Not so the theorist or teacher! He desires to strengthen the intuitive sense of form by conscious analysis, and he believes that such analysis, either intuitive or conscious, is necessary for composer, performer, and listener alike. The ability to understand intuitively the musical rhetoric of the last century may be the inheritance of the average listener of today, but it is in dealing with contemporaneous music in any period that analysis is most needed, although it is then most difficult and indeed hazardous. At best, theory and appreciative analysis must follow creation at a respectful distance, but it *must* follow — for the sake of the art itself as well as for our own sakes; and it should be the endeavor of theorists and public alike to reduce the distance which separates the two processes to a minimum.

Even the composer who places the greatest reliance upon an intuitive sense of form inherits from the past a certain accumulation of theory, the result of analysis. He is not forced to compose in all the styles and forms of preceding periods. In a sense he recapitulates the entire history of his art, and by plotting this curve of development in his own musical experience he is able to take the next step which this curve points out to him. Analysis of the music he is hearing or writing is a constant condition of the act, and, while we may not all be gifted with this ability, psychologists are agreed that many processes may be transferred to subconscious intuition from conscious thought. Our aim, then, is not analysis as an end in itself but as a means of strengthening the intuitive sense of form.

For the interpreter of modern music, a knowledge of its

forms is indispensable, though he is less interested in methods than in 'results.' The relation of punctuation to declamation needs little proof; after all, a musical performance is a species of 'elocution.' The reader of a speech usually expects to find his periods in their right locations; but the musician cannot always depend upon his printed phrasing. There can be no doubt that the interpretation of a composition is affected by our idea of its structure and rhetoric, but we should scarcely expect an actor to make himself understood in a language in which he could not tell subject from predicate. That our musical performances are not poorer than they are must be due to the fact that we cannot live with a composition long enough to be able to pronounce the musical words without acquiring some understanding of what the music has to say. Analysis for the interpreter should confirm and strengthen this understanding of the musical rhetoric.

If the innate feeling for form were not possessed by all to some degree, the audiences in our concert halls would be much smaller. But difficulty of coördinating details in music which reaches the ear as a rapid succession of sounds has increased in this generation because the marks of musical punctuation have been radically changed. This is the reason why so many in our audiences come to the close of a modern work somewhat 'out-of-breath,' asking what it is all about. They find the music chaotic because they have overlooked many points at which a 'mental breath' should have been taken. It is with these newer methods of integration that analysis of contemporaneous music has to deal.

Analysis of form has a place, therefore, in the education of a musician or lover of music; and courses which handle the material in a modern spirit, akin to that of scientific research, should be found in our musical curricula. Too often there has been a tendency to present the subject only as it relates to the most 'formal' music of the classical or early romantic periods. In some institutions teaching of the rudiments of form has been combined with elementary appreciation courses which give the only introduction to the subject. And it has been handled solely in connection with work in composition: a student studying a form and then writing in that form. Undoubtedly, in the ideal musical education with all departments of musicianship developed simultaneously, the training of eyes, ears and fingers, and the study of counterpoint and harmony as two sides of the same process, creative work in Form and Composition as analysis and synthesis is the best possible method of teaching. Unfortunately it is not always practicable, and in the case of some students who can never compose in the larger forms it is impossible.

There is a genuine need for an advanced course in Form and Analysis in which the details of the subject can be examined in the musical 'laboratory' by students who are ready to form independent judgments. Such a course would become the basis, consciously or unconsciously, for criticism and genuine appreciation in after-life. It would vitally affect and mold the interpretation of future performances. And it is unlikely to harm the future composer (in spite of the distrust of musical pedagogy in certain quarters), provided the subject is taught with due regard for the opinions of all and with a real love for freedom and the variety that results therefrom in this freest of arts. Dogmatism is decidedly out of place in the teaching of formal principles; opposition to the subject as such has been due largely to the lack of flexibility in teaching methods. There must be regard for the integrity of the music, the individuality of each composition, and the freedom of the composer. The rhetoric of music cannot be studied apart from content; so for the advanced student the best method is that of the research laboratory.

A thorough knowledge of harmony including its most advanced vocabulary is a prerequisite, because modern harmony has a direct bearing upon modern form. A detailed study of the history of music should have provided the student with the historical point of view and the conviction that form did not begin and end with the 'Classical' school. The ability to read at sight is essential, as each student must analyze for himself and should be able to read the more complicated arrangements of modern music at least to his own satisfaction. With this equipment the laboratory method can be used from the very beginning of the study. Methods of analysis must be tested again in the light of recent developments. The class is given a body of material which it is to dissect in its own way and the findings are then considered in group discussions with arguments advanced pro and con. Then it is by no means necessary to arrive at a decision based upon a majority opinion or announced *ex cathedra*. Two analyses equally valid may be defended, with the discussion assuming the character of a debate. The teacher should be careful not to force his own conclusions upon the students, but should assist in the sifting of evidence and the weighing of arguments.

The great need is a training of the ability to discover what actually exists in the music itself. The 'name' or label of the condition or form is relatively unimportant. Disputes over classification have often involved the most prominent theorists of form and have been influential in bringing the whole subject into disrepute. As a matter of fact, a resulting difference of opinion has nothing to do with the benefits to be derived from the process of analysis and does not affect the value of the subject in the least. If the student is already familiar with the usual forms and their hybrids found as movements of multiple forms, it adds greatly to his interest and pleasure to analyze such works with no *a priori* indication of the form he will find in any movement. This is vastly better than asking the student to analyze a number of movements that he knows in advance will illustrate a certain general form.

It is not possible, of course, to avoid technical considerations in this study. Nor is it desirable. The more thorough the musical preparation and experience, the easier the approach to a new composition. It is quite possible on the other hand to write of style in music, to discuss the impressionism or expressionism, the philosophy or theosophy of modern music, without approaching very near to the problems of the music itself. We have had many such more-or-less hermeneutic interpretations of modern music and much propaganda written both for and against certain composers or works, but we often finish the reading of such presentations with the feeling that little has been said that speaks directly of the musical rhetoric. It is the author's belief that the general reader as well as the special student of music may be interested in the problems of analysis. Although this preface has dealt with the method of approach in the classroom, the suggestions in it can be used with some modification by the individual who wishes to make his own study of modern music. They also serve to indicate the spirit in which the writer undertakes to examine contemporaneous compositions for their evidences of form.

CHANGING FORMS IN MODERN MUSIC

CHAPTER I

WHAT HAS HAPPENED TO MUSIC?

If some misfortune had prevented our hearing any music written during the twentieth century, and we were now to be introduced for the first time to compositions representative of the ultra-modern idiom, our first reaction would probably be both question and exclamation: "What has happened to music!?" This is a perfectly natural response and should not occasion surprise or resentment in the friends of modern music who sponsored the introduction, for we only acknowledge in this way the unique character of music as an art.

It is the glory as well as the paradox of music that it may be the oldest and, at the same time, the youngest of the arts. By its very nature it is destined to be ever changing, and so, ever young. Theorists may set up distinctions between objective and subjective music, but the truth is that there is *no* objective music. The art itself is subjective in its very being, and this may be the reason why it seems to renew its youth in every generation.

The Golden Age of this art is not back in the days of ancient Greece, although the 'opera' of Sophocles and Euripides furnished the inspiration of the Florentine rediscovery of opera in 1600. The creative musician is not confronted by compositions in his field that have presented an objective reality, in such form that the composition remains challenging in its approach to perfection, as the creative artist, working with visible forms in space, is confronted with the human body in Greek sculpture. The painter has his Golden Age of the Renaissance — or earlier, depending upon his tastes and preferences. At about the same time, the school of Palestrina was creating music of great beauty.

While we are making more and more of this music accessible in print and in performance, and acknowledge its beauty, the music of Palestrina does not challenge the composer of the present day in the same way that the canvases of the Renaissance challenge the painter, because music is not to the same degree an objective art.

Musicians agree that the years which produced the monumental fugues of Bach were 'golden years.' The general public might be more inclined to so characterize the later rococo period, the classicism of Mozart, or the romanticism of Beethoven. Do not these preferences indicate the mood of the public appreciation, rather than establish any hierarchy of values? May we perhaps be living in a 'golden age,' or must we wait, look forward to some future period and resign ourselves to the idea that we are living in a period of 'transition'? The historian whose research has given him a more detailed acquaintance with some other period or composer will be enthusiastic over the compositions in his special field; or his more eclectic taste may include an appreciation of many styles. Each period, he may state, presents absolute values, which cannot be compared for the reason that there is no objective reality to which the compositions of different periods may be referred.

Before we look at some of the more radical features of contemporaneous music, which seem to break with all traditions of the art, we need to reconsider our attitude of approach and ask ourselves what may be a reasonable basis for our hopes or fears for modern music. There are two points of view which, it seems to me, we should avoid if possible. One is the idea that the history of music presents a continuous evolution always to a higher level of quality and style, and that the new is necessarily the best. The other extreme would be to insist that the music of all periods and all races is of equal merit. Is not a third position tenable? This would be a statement of the faith that a genius can find expression in any period and style, and that he will so use materials and style as to express not only himself but his time.

This is but another way of saying that the idea is more important than the vocabulary. We shall consider what is involved in the acceptance of this position in a later chapter. In an approach to modern music itself it means the simple acknowledgment of the character of the art. The very elements of life, the dynamics of motion and sound, are used subjectively for a new expression. Music must express in a peculiar way the age in which we live, or our age will remain forever inarticulate. Life receives a new interpretation. The musical vocabulary and the style of coloratura opera are quite different from that of the Wagnerian music-drama, yet we are tempted to acknowledge that a great composer has just as wide a range of expression and characterization in the one style as in the other. The musical vocabulary changes; new harmonic idioms appear; certain progressions 'date themselves'; certain effects are even considered the 'property' of individual composers. We must realize that in all this there is something more fundamental than vocabulary, and we should not allow the difficulties of the modern harmony to distract our attention from the underlying problems of the musical rhetoric.

It is true that there have been remarkable changes in the 'sound' of our music in the last few decades. Chords have been constructed upon the basis of seconds, until they look like bunches of grapes on the modern score. These are found not only in Piano tone-clusters where one may use his fist, his arm, or a stick of wood, but in the refined idiom of a String Quartet (*Illustration* No. 1). Superstructures of fourths or fifths (*Illustration* No. 2), or chord masses based upon no apparent principle (the first chord of *Illustration* No. 3), increase the dissonance. Two or more tonalities are used simultaneously (*Illustration* No. 4), and polytonality piles up six harmonic planes in the following Illustration (No. 5). Atonal music, in which all reference to tonal centers is abandoned, presents its special problems of punctuation, which will be considered later. It seems to avoid with special care any combination which, by association or inference of any sort, might hark back to a tonic key (*Illustration* No. 6). The result is an unbroken succession of dissonance.

3

ILLUSTRATION Nº1

BÉLA BARTÓK
Fourth Quartet
First Movement
Measure 13

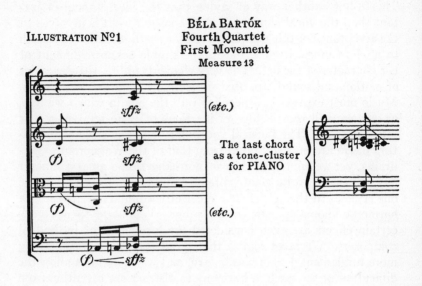

The last chord
as a tone-cluster
for PIANO

ALEXANDER SCRIABIN (Op. 53)
Fifth Sonata for Piano
Measure 268
ILLUSTRATION Nº2 *poco rit.*

ILLUSTRATION №3

LEO ORNSTEIN
From Opus 41, №4
(For Piano — <u>Two</u> Hands!)

NOTE: Each accidental in the above Illustration (№3) refers to the note which it precedes and to that note alone.

ILLUSTRATION № 4

ARTHUR HONEGGER
First Sonata (1917)
For Violin and Piano
End of Second Movement

ILLUSTRATION Nº 5

DARIUS MILHAUD
Sonata for Piano (1916)
Second Movement
Measures 203-212

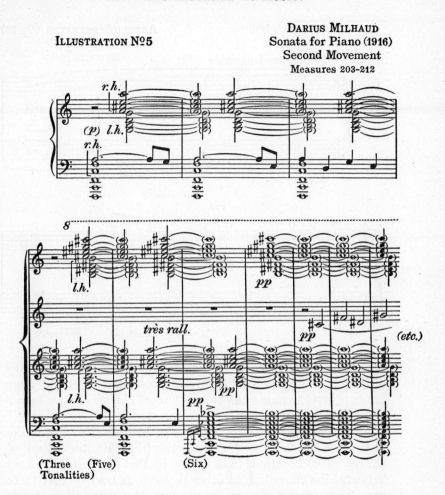

(Three   (Five)   (Six)
Tonalities)

These idioms may seem strange, particularly if our musical experience has been provided by programs chosen almost exclusively from the music of past generations; but, as the strangeness of the new vocabulary gradually disappears with acquaintance, we may find that here are musical values not so radically different

ILLUSTRATION № 6

ARNOLD SCHOENBERG (Op. 25)
Suite: Gigue
Measures 40-42

Noch etwas langsamer

in character from those of the past; and, as we trace the evidences of form in the newer rhetoric, we will come to realize that what has happened to music has been a gradual change of style rather than a revolution.

Only the future historians of this period, with the perspective of time, will be able to decide whether the 'ultramodernism' of our day should continue to be known by that term after the word 'modern' has moved on to other periods. It may be that there have been greater changes in the last fifty years than at any other period since the *nuove musiche*, or New Music, of 1600, which we still call by that name.[1] To some listeners, to-day, the use of dissonance appears excessive and beyond all reason; but we must

---

[1] Those who look for cycles of similar length in history may note *ars nova* approximately three hundred years earlier, and affirm that 1900 was foreordained as the appropriate date for 'New Music' to reappear as an historical term.

not forget that the ear has a wonderful capacity to receive and assimilate sounds more and more complex. Critics of the new vocabulary may insist that there is a difference between getting used to a dissonance and admitting its musical value — as we may get used to the sound of an elevated railroad but not admit its æsthetic beauty. Modern composers, however, apparently have faith in the ability of the listener to follow them in the enjoyment of more and more dissonant combinations; and it must be acknowledged that, as in the fairy tale of 'Beauty and the Beast' which Ravel includes in *Ma mère l'oye*, if we only believe in this 'Beast' who appears so dissonant and ugly, he often changes before our eyes and ears into a charming prince.

But without any special pleading for the new music at this point, it must be admitted that our reception of anything new depends upon certain conditions. First and most important in music, there should be an opportunity for the repeated hearings that are necessary for any real understanding. We must realize that the habits of long and intimate acquaintance have already predisposed most of us in favor of the music we know so well. We intuitively understand its integration; and its vocabulary is so familiar that the rhetoric of its expression can produce an emotional response in us. The effort of conscious analysis is most necessary in approach to contemporaneous music in which the legerdemain of colorful, kaleidoscopic harmonies, may prevent our recognizing the underlying structure.

Then, we must lay aside as far as possible any prejudices we may have. This means that we should accept the music as a sincere expression of the composer, and attempt to appreciate it on its own merits. In other words, we should not continue the mistake of judging Wagner by the standards of Mozart. Of course, each listener brings to the hearing his previous musical experience of few or many years, and he brings also a certain disposition or temperament, somewhat dependent upon the number of these years. All of this will influence his reception of new musical experiences, and properly should do so. Modern music does not ask for a surrender of all the rights of the listener, of his individuality, and the right of private judgment. Just how far a reasonable æsthetic theory may adapt standards to changing conditions will be considered in the next chapter. This music merely asks that it may not suffer from prejudgment, which, of course, is no judgment. Prejudgments result from prejudices like those of the German conservative who sees in modern music the downfall of German imperialism and the dangerous rise of American democracy.[1] Still, the music section of an exhibit, opened by the Nazi government in Frankfurt to show 'horrible examples' of modern art, had to be closed, it is said, because people came not to laugh but to listen and enjoy. Others see in modern music a direct attack upon the rights of property, because the rights of the tonic of the musical scale are no longer respected! It is this type of prejudice, transferring political views of economic theories from the world of reality to the purely subjective world of music, that should be avoided if we are to approach modern music with an open mind.

It may seem unnecessary to preface a technical consideration of musical rhetoric with a plea for an 'open mind'; but it is surprising how much of the literature in the field exhibits prejudices more or less openly expressed. May we not expect to find at least a faith in the integrity of the art itself and a willingness to acknowledge the probability that a composer, who is trying to give form to his musical ideas, is sincere in so doing? It is then our duty to discover the threads of development which give continuity to the musical process, to seek for evidences of form where the old landmarks are missing. The music has been written. We may attempt to close our ears to it, fearing that music is on the return to barbarism; but in so doing we shall be living our musical lives apart from our own generation, and shall lose to that extent the enjoyment of a very fascinating and interesting present. The creative artist does not face the past. He conceives or hears

---

[1] Heinrich Schenker, *Erläuterungs-Ausgabe der Letzten Fünf Sonaten Beethoven* (Opus 101, pp. 19–26).

a new music and, by bringing to bear all his power upon the work at hand, produces this in a synthesis or form. If he theorizes, his theory and his practice are not always in agreement. Usually he merely asks us to listen to something that he has heard and that he believes is beautiful.

The professional critic attempts an estimate in the light of his experience. The theorist may be of some assistance, though he is often tardy in offering it. He attempts to explain the work in its totality, or to systematize its methods in a particular direction; but he never fully succeeds in doing so, for in his analysis something of the spirit escapes from the body; and methods thus discovered cannot synthetically and mechanically produce masterpieces, any more than a knowledge of chemical combinations can enable the scientist in the laboratory to produce a living body. Both critic and theorist may help us to understand, but nothing can take the place of a thorough personal acquaintance with the music itself. We must give the music of our generation a hearing on its own merits.

The next generation fortunately, we discover then, does not have to begin where we began. Whatever the decision of biologists concerning the inheritance of acquired tastes, it is certainly a fact that succeeding generations have been able to perceive, identify, and 'appreciate' musical sounds of increasing intricacy. As a corollary to that fact, the child prodigy of to-day composes not in the idiom of Mozart but in that of Stravinsky. The ready response of those who criticize modern music is that babes in arms can pound out tone-clusters — improvising with their fists on the keyboard — and so may be considered budding composers; but again, this is confusing vocabulary with rhetoric, and, of course, has nothing to do with the process of composition.

What we do have a right to expect and demand in a musical composition, based upon a possible minimum of æsthetic theory, will be discussed in the next chapter. The remaining chapters will then present a more detailed answer to the question, "What has happened to music?" An answer, necessarily incomplete and inconclusive, can be given here. What has happened to music is merely what we should expect to happen in a subjective art. The vocabulary and methods of expression have changed, but the essential character of the art remains unchanged. There has been a normal evolution — in a rapid tempo, to be sure — during the last few decades, but not revolution. The term 'evolution' does not necessarily include a claim for progressively superior attainments in art. It simply means there have been changes whereby we can have the music that best expresses our own day and generation.

CHAPTER II

ÆSTHETICS OF A CHANGING STANDARD

Æsthetics, as a designation of a specific field in the philosophy of art, is little more than a hundred years old, but the question 'What is Beauty?' is much older; in fact, it is a part of the central philosophical problem. Without attempting a detailed presentation of the various theories in what has been called the 'nightmare' subject of æsthetics, let us consider a minimum of theory that may serve as a basis for our study of modern music. What we seek is a short creed of beauty, freed, if possible, from all dogmatism and the changing conventions of fashion. But is such a creed possible? How may we give up our hold upon an inflexible, dogmatic standard, and not find ourselves at once lost in a flux of sound?

Paradoxical as the concept may appear in words, what we require is a changing standard. A recognition of this standard requires that we differentiate, in any definition of art, two elements: one, the material or vocabulary, and the other, the form or rhetoric. The acceptance of a changing standard is a recognition of the fact that materials change, that they are different in each art, and that they are different in every period of an art like music, while the principles of form, expressed by means of these different materials, remain. Even the most aphoristic definition, "Art is Man added to Nature," includes these two elements, the one as varied as nature itself and the materials of the universe, and the other, selective, arranging these materials in a new order.

It is always necessary for the artist to give form to the material he selects. This demands the hard travail of labor as well as the original joy of conception. In a sense, form is the penalty all things must pay for the privilege of existing. That is, it brings with it of necessity certain limitations which the artist cannot escape, because it represents the only basis for communication of æsthetic emotion.

A work of art presents a new expression of some relationship of unity in variety, a new variation on this world-old theme. It is the discovery of these relationships which analysis attempts. In music this is especially difficult, because form seems so inextricably linked with content. In contemporaneous music, form, or structure, does not appear to be a conspicuous feature, at first hearing.[1] There have been periods in which certain facets of the art have received more attention than others; successive epochs have stressed rhythmic, melodic, or harmonic elements. Theoretically, all of these have existed from the beginning, the harmonic concept being inherent in a melodic line, and the melodic concept, a result of rhythmic accent. We have just passed through a period in which all three elements have united in emphasizing the formal integration, so that, by contrast, the music of the present period may appear formless. To-day, our attention is attracted by the new discoveries of harmony, and by a bewildering counterpointing of rhythmic patterns. The interest is in color rather than in line; while all elements, color, harmony, and rhythm, have grown increasingly dissonant.

We are apt to criticize this music for its lack of form, or praise it for its freedom from form, depending upon our point of view; but we should refrain from taking either position until we have subjected the work to a thorough analysis, realizing that form in music is continuously important, and never more so than at those periods in which evidences of form are most difficult to discover. If melody, harmony, and rhythm do not join in the punctuation of the form, then we must seek for the evidences of form in each, separately. If we cannot find coördination at one level in the structure, then we must look for it at another. If the older theory no longer holds in certain situations, then we must change methods, and rewrite our theory to meet the new developments.

[1] I once heard George Whiting in a lecture at Harvard say that modern music was suffering from rickets.

With a changing standard, the analyst, who seeks for evidences of form in every possible way, may still defend his position. Can we say as much for the theorist who attempts to define or set limits to a special musical vocabulary? Is there such a thing as a restricted 'poetic' vocabulary in music? Can we say that these sounds are beautiful and may be used, while those are not? Shall the limit in the size of modern note-clusters be set by the human hand, or shall we allow the composer to direct the performer to cut for himself a piece of wood of a certain length the better to 'play' still larger clusters? With the composition of music for mechanical instruments, there is nothing to prevent the composer from calling for all the notes of the piano-keyboard at the same time. Absurd as these extremes may seem, when we are asked if a composer has a right to use these materials, there is only one answer that can be defended. The artist has the right to do so, and he should, if he feels he must. A master, like the Christian, is above Law, in the Biblical sense. And yet the work of art has law, a law of its own being, if it is, indeed, art.

Having granted this right, what defense have we from the assaults upon our ear, upon our present standards of taste? We may deny the importance of mere vocabulary, and then seek to discover what the composer has to say. We cannot refuse him the right to express himself as he pleases, but we have a right to ask ourselves if what the artist pleases to do, pleases us. Then we must hasten to define this word 'pleasure' with all the connotations of a term in æsthetics. Art does not have to be pretty. It does not have to entertain. It must be true, even if brutally dissonant. It must 'please God' and the god and the artist in each one of us. Time, the greatest art-critic, alone can decide.

But if we are not satisfied with such generalizations, and try to state in less rhetorical terms what it is that produces æsthetic pleasure, we have difficulty in defining it. Some would call it style, or even 'message,' carefully explaining different points of view in their use of these terms. It is, without question, the basis upon which the future will accept or reject the music of this generation when the superficialities of vocabulary no longer distract attention, but it is difficult to define. We may be sure, however, that it has some relation to the principles of form. If a composer is to be articulate, his music must have some articulation or integration. The old marks of punctuation by means of harmonic cadences may disappear, but some type of periodicity remains, and this is capable of analysis.

When we say this, we are not forced to take the position that this beauty of form appeals only to the intellect. It gives æsthetic pleasure because it appeals in a direct way to the æsthetic emotion. We expect the author of *Form in Music*, Stewart Macpherson, to divide the appeals which music makes into three: physical, emotional, and mental; and then to state unhesitatingly that the mental appeal is the most important. On the other hand, one who is concerned with the 'appreciation' of the art may refuse to accept this order and, using a Socratian dichotomy, may divide the emotional appeal into that of the higher and lower emotions, placing this newly defined and elevated emotional appeal above the mental. Again, if we carefully guard the use of the word 'message,' ridding it of all didactic preachments, it may approach the idea for which we are seeking. Through whatever channel beauty reaches the spirit — be it physical, mental, or emotional — the most important feature of æsthetic gratification is our response to the selective creation of the artist, and in this response, form, in all the larger meaning of that term, is more important than material. To state that form has only a mental appeal and then, as a believer in the prime importance of form, to be forced to place this appeal first, is to limit our position unnecessarily. Form has a physical and emotional appeal as well as a mental approach.

Whatever æsthetic theory we may hold, the demand for form cannot be denied. Let us include in the musician's vocabulary every word imaginable and those as yet undreamed of; let us include all the material from racial scales unlike our own, or from scales manufactured synthetically. Add to these all the harmonic combinations on a quarter-tone instrument, or one with infinitely smaller gradations. Put all these together and we have only a dictionary. Admit to any art the free choice of material and the problem of its handling still remains. It is true that in music, more than in any other art, the idea *is* the form; dealing in intangibles, it is very difficult, if not impossible, to separate the two. But in this work we are placing the emphasis upon the rhetoric of music in phrase, sentence, or paragraph, rather than on the separate words.

If we attempt to interpret our changing standard as it relates to this rhetoric, we find two crucial points of attack, two points at which we cannot surrender if we are to discover any unity in the use of this variety of materials which we have just admitted to be infinite in variation: first, there must be some differentiation of materials. In music this may mean a differentiation in quality or value: scale-tones versus non-scale tones; chord-tones versus non-chordal tones; tones belonging to a given theme versus those which are not found there. Or the differentiation may be one of quantity: accent versus non-accent, and so on. In some way a variety of values must be established, for it is only by some such differentiation that the first step in construction can be taken. A single tone or beat remains in static unity until another tone or beat is differentiated, or until this tone or beat detaches itself and begins an activity or motion that can only be satisfied by some type of repetition or return which completes the circle of form at a higher level in the structure. This return is our second point.

We may fail to recognize that these two requirements are met in some particular modern composition unless we realize in the first place that the establishment of a differentiation in values has now become in many cases an individual matter. Formerly, we could refer to a pre-established scale. Relationships of harmonies were recognized as a standard of exchange. They had a currency, we may say, that was universally accepted, at least in the Occident. What has happened in music to-day can be compared to what occurs in a country where the old currency is no longer accepted. It is as if each composer were forced to establish his own coinage. The differentiation of material may be upon a different basis in the case of different composers or, in the case of the same composer, at different periods; the basis for differentiation may even change with each composition. This makes the exploration of modern music extremely difficult. We must pass these custom boundaries and accept the currency of the country we enter if we are to enjoy the beauties of its new tonal landscapes.

Our second point of attack, the repetition which rounds out the circle of form in modern compositions, is more disguised, more varied, and thus more difficult to recognize than ever before. Not only is repetition disguised in the most distant variation, but it occurs at the most irregular intervals of time; it is asymmetrically spaced, not in the neat parallels to which we have been accustomed. Yet it is this very irregularity which, consciously or unconsciously perceived, gives the music its individual charm. We enjoy the irregular more than the regular when we understand it.

Perhaps there is need to remind those who are setting up new standards of values, new scales of differentiation in place of the old harmonic relationships, that a new and individual coinage can be accepted only if its use is repeated. For instance, if a composer wishes to take the twelve notes of the chromatic or duo-decuple scale, and, without relating them to the focal-points, tonic, dominant, etc., selects a new arrangement for a particular composition — calling that his structural principle, or motive, and using it as a basis of differentiation,— there must be sufficient repetition of this structure to give it validity or currency. As we shall see in a later chapter, Schoenberg uses this method in atonal music; but he satisfies this requirement of repetition, repeating one formula, **A**, for instance (*Illustration* No. 7) more than twenty times under various disguises in the twenty-four measures of the *Præludium* of his *Suite für Klavier* (Opus 25).

ILLUSTRATION № 7

ARNOLD SCHOENBERG
From Opus 25

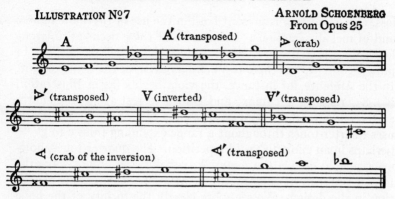

There are composers who state quite frankly that they wish to escape from the obligation of repetition in any degree. But, usually, this is more emphatically expressed in the statement than in their music. Let us consider, as a typical case, Alois Hába's claim that in his *Second String Quartet* he has arrived at a style distinguished "by free arrangement of the thoughts, by the complete lack of repetition or of transposition of shorter fractional parts."[1] When we examine his Quartet we find, neverthe-

ILLUSTRATION № 8

ALOIS HÁBA
Second Quarter-tone
Quartet for Strings

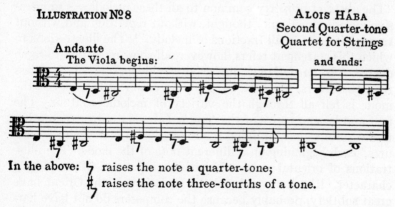

In the above: ♭ raises the note a quarter-tone;
♯ raises the note three-fourths of a tone.

[1] Alois Hába: *Von der Psychologie der Musikalischen Gestaltung*, (p. 51). "Sie zeichnet sich durch freie Anordnung der Gedanken und durch das gänzliche Fehlen der Widerholung oder der Transposition kürzerer Bruchstücke aus."

less, that repetition is present both in the use of rhythmic figures and of melodic fractions. It is true that these occur at different levels in the structure; there is not the usual parallelism in phrase-content, but there is much repetition of the beat-content. In the Andante, for instance, the viola begins (as in Illustration No. 8), rises to a climax, and comes to rest again on c-sharp, at the end. In the sixty-two measures of this movement Hába uses quarter-tones throughout a range extending from c to g″ — perhaps in an effort to avoid repetition. The quarter-tones, however, merely double the material available and do not solve the formal problem of constructing a melody without some repetition in the design. We see more clearly the futility of the hope that any composer may escape from the fundamental obligations of form in the illustrations which Hába gives as a basis for his style. He believes that he has discovered this progressive melody without repetitions in certain Czech folk-songs, in old Chorals, in a *Graduale* of the eleventh century, and in the 'Hymn of St. John,' the *Sancta Johannes*, from which our **ut-re-mi** is derived. He points out that all of these have a character essentially different from that of European music for the last three hundred years: "The abstract property common to all these melodies is progressive melodic (melismic) thought, without repetition and without transposition of small fractions of melody."[1] The illustrations to which this statement refers, however, all show repetition to some degree. The Gregorian examples, as would be expected, show less than the others, but here the unifying power of the final of the mode is felt all through the variety of melodic contour. The first and last measures of the *Sancta Johannes* mirror each other to a certain extent, unifying the succession of intervening 'measures,' each beginning on a different note of the mode. The illustrations of oriental music also exhibit repetition of a different character. Rhythmic and melodic variations in the Orient have great subtlety, probably because the composers do not have har-

[1] (*Ibid.*, p. 42.) "Die allen diesen Melodien gemeinsame abstrachte Eigenschaft ist das *melische Vorwärtsdenken*, ohne Wiederholung und ohne Transponierung kleiner melodischer Bruchteile."

monic channels for emotional expression; and there is much that reminds us of the Orient in the asymmetrical forms of modern music. But these forms are not without repetitions. In the following illustration, which is quoted by Hába, the writer has indicated some of the numerous "repetitions of melodic fractions." (*Illustration* No. 9.) The chorals cited by Hába contain so many

ILLUSTRATION №9   TURKISH FOLK-SONG*
(Hornbostel's Collection)

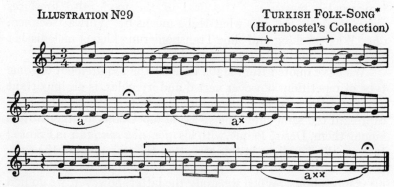

The arrows, brackets, and letters indicate relationships.

* Quoted by Alois Hába in *Von der Psychologie der Musikalischen Gestaltung* (p. 40).

repetitions that it is scarcely possible to indicate them all. The following is typical. (*Illustration* No. 10.)

ILLUSTRATION №10   FRENCH CHORAL*
(*Comenius,* — Psalm 130)

* Quoted by Alois Hába (*ibid.*, p. 39).

Note the answering rhythms of the first measure with the third, and of the second with the fourth. The third and fourth measures, and the seventh and eighth measures, rhyme. The end of the second measure answers the end of the first by inversion. Although two of the measures vary from the uniform size of five units, they are in **six** and **four**, so the total is the same as that of two regular measures. The final of the mode also produces unity of effect. If this is what Hába means by "Vorwärtsdenken, ohne Wiederholung und ohne Transponierung kleiner melodischer Bruchteile," certainly no one would object.

We have quoted from Hába because the requirement of some type of repetition, however varied and irregular, is an important point of attack in modern music. There are others who have expressed the same intention to avoid repetitions in other words; among them, Désiré Paque, with his *ajonction constante* in France.[1] It is usually found, as in this case, that the statement of the composer's intention in words is more radical than its evidence in his compositions. When we study the latter, however, we do find that a clear distinction must be made between repetition which occurs in regular parallels — somewhat like the balanced lines of verse — and that which occurs with the irregular freedom usually associated with prose. With the exception of the French Choral, above, which exhibits clear parallelism in structure, the other illustrations do point the way to a style which departs from the regular constructions of most European music for the last few hundred years. It is for the historian to indicate the sources of the more regular style in the regularity of the dance patterns of Western Europe, or in the regularity of the Court and formal society during this period; it is for the psychologist to consider how fundamental and deep-rooted this demand for parallelism may be. Does it result from the inhibitions of civilization, or should we recognize in it the natural expression of man as a bilateral being with a certain parallelism of structure? The musical imagination, however, should not be fettered in the

[1] Cf. *Notre Esthétique*, in **La Revue Musicale**, February, 1930.

regularity of poetic rhythms, if the musical idea demands the freedom of prose. Modern composers, in any case, have succeeded in breaking away from the symmetrical structures of recurring balancing phrases, and are writing in a style which does bear some resemblance to Gregorian or Oriental melody.

To Hába, the discovery of his new style seems like a 'second birth.' He remembers that, as a youth, he improvised on his violin (in the evening, before his mother set a light in their little room) just such expressions of a free, unbound soul. Then, for a time, he attempted to fit his thought in the channel of older forms, and only recently has he returned to his earlier freedom of expression. Improvisation, not as it was formerly cultivated at the key-board, but on paper, seems to be the ideal of several modern composers. No doubt even the youthful fancies of a composer of Hába's gifts would have had some artistic value, had his early improvisations been captured by some hidden reproducing machine; but their value, the theorist continues to assert, would be in direct relation to an inner coherency of thought, expressed, it is true, with a certain freedom, but made cogent by some unity however subtle and even unrecognized by the improvisor.

Modern music, then, may strive for and acclaim freedom in form, but not complete freedom from form. There remain the two requirements for the production of any form: some differentiation of materials, and some relation of these differentiated materials by repetition. It is impossible to establish the differentiation without the repetition. Conversely, repetitions cannot be set up in a chaos of materials without a differentiation of values. This is the dilemma of the modern composer: how to become eloquent with an irregularity of rhetoric which will approach the continuity of good prose in tonal material, when differentiated values tend to disappear with increasing dissonance. The moving rhetoric of the first Chopin *Prelude*, for instance, is made possible because certain harmonic values point to the final C-major goal. One of the first results of an abandonment of tonality before substitute bases of differentiation were set up, was a greater dependence upon repetition, so we had the situation that composers were writing with an extremely dissonant or atonal vocabulary, but with bald repetitions of four-measure phrases and a poverty of rhetoric, writing 'modern music' in a style more regular than that of the most 'formal' period of the eighteenth century.[1]

This extreme regularity was not obvious at once because our attention was distracted by the sounds of the new musical words. We may even suppose that this regularity is necessary while the public is busy assimilating the new vocabulary.

To illustrate the relationship between these two formal principles, which we retain amid changing standards, we may use the kaleidoscope. Here a chance grouping of colors in forms, by repetition in mirrors, produces a design. By such repetition, anything appears to be justified. C. H. Wilkinson, in *Harmonic and Keyboard Designing*, using parts of *God Save the King*, carries this idea a step further, and studies music as a source of design to be used, for instance, for the manufacture of textiles. He produces mechanically many such designs from a single piece of music by selecting any unit and reducing it to a graph somewhat like that of a piano-player roll; but to produce his final design in each case, he repeats, inverts, mirrors, or mitres this unit. He believes that designers who are at a loss for ideas have only to turn to music to find an unlimited number of new designs. It is the repetition, however, which makes the form in this case. Some modern music seems to be constructed on the same principle — any combination appearing to be justified if repeated. The real problems occur when the repetition is neither immediate nor regular. We must discover the design in a continuous process which takes the graph of an entire composition as a basis, and does not arbitrarily mirror fragments of material, as in a kaleidoscope.

[1] Cf. my outline of Ornstein's *Poems of 1917* in the **Musical Quarterly**, April, 1921.

A study of the rhetoric of music is therefore an investigation of the newer methods of securing cogency in musical expression, the different ways in which these two fundamentals, differentiations of values and their repetitions, are secured.

Analysis, either conscious or intuitive, should be the basis for all genuine criticism; but criticism with its expression of an opinion as to the quality or value of a process or a composition is something more than analysis. When the analyst ventures an opinion as to the value of the material analyzed, or the processes discovered,— in a word, when he indicates the direction of this evolution as progressive or retrogressive,— he should realize that he is leaving one field and entering another. The analyst and the true critic are one in the sense that both must admit the freedom of form in music, while they demand some evidence of form as in any art creation. In thus defending a constantly 'changing standard,' their position is all the stronger for any retreat; and what might be made the cruel vivisection of contemporary art-works becomes a way to sympathetic understanding.

CHAPTER III

THE MUSICAL SENTENCE
AND ITS HARMONIC PUNCTUATION

Having suggested the spirit in which we should approach a study of modern music, and having reduced our æsthetic 'baggage' to a minimum, we are ready to leave such generalities for a consideration of particular methods. If form in music results from "the determination of definite tonal complexes, larger or smaller, within a musical organism,"[1] we must set limits to the complexes before we can compare and relate them. Here we face the subject-object problem in philosophy, and this problem in turn depends for its solution upon psychology. Whatever we are able to take as a whole becomes by this very act 'formed,' that is, a recognized unit or formal element, for us.[2] Does this avoidance of the philosophical problem leave us with nothing but subjective verdicts as varied as the individuals reporting? We believe this is not the case, and the validity of our belief will depend upon the amount of agreement that results from the analysis of modern music. What we are seeking are evidences of form. Evidence that is valid should convince at least a majority of the hearers, and can then be accepted as 'true.'

There would seem to be two paths of approach to any composition; we may proceed from the whole to its smallest parts, or from the smallest unit to the whole. In this chapter neither of these paths will be entered at its logical beginning. Rather we shall attempt to set off a unit, between these two extremes, the musical *sentence*, and then discuss its appearance and changing

---

[1] H. Erpf, *Der Begriff der Musikalischen Form.*

[2] The listener is influenced in his action by relationships existing in the nature of the physical material (simple vibrational ratios, etc.), by the history of organization within the art, by his own personal experience in general, and by that part of his experience in the immediate past, represented by the sounds already heard in the particular composition.

punctuation in modern music. This has the advantage of presenting periodicity in convenient lengths, the punctuation of which has changed so gradually that we may have some hope of following the process. By a re-definition of the musical sentence we may succeed in retaining that unit for the analysis of music in which the phrase alone seems at first glance the sole unit of organization. A determination of the melodic inflection of the phrase follows in the next chapter, and, after that, the measure and its rhythmic generation will be considered.

These are not three unrelated subjects, although it is true that the burden of formal organization is often carried in modern music by one of the three: by repetition of harmonic masses in cadential punctuation, or by melodic inflection, or by self-generating rhythm, with relatively less help from the other two than is the case in earlier music, where all three combine to reinforce the punctuation. (*Illustration* No. 11.) These three chapters will be concerned with the same problem which received theoretical consideration in Chapter II, namely, repetition or relationship in some degree between two structural features. They approach the problem at different levels in the structure represented by the technical terms: musical sentence, phrase, and motive. Then our direction will be reversed, and forms larger than the monoform period will be examined as they appear in modern music.

To what extent can the methods used in the musical analysis of sentences in the nineteenth century be used in the twentieth? It will be necessary to review these briefly.[1] The terms used have been borrowed from the terminology of other arts. The graphic presentation of musical architecture has been used effectively by the Russian, Conus,[2] and other designs appear in

[1] Some of the important texts are: E. Prout, *Musical Form, Applied Form;* Bussler, *Musikalische Formenlehre;* Stewart Macpherson, *Form in Music;* Hugo Riemann, *System der musikalischen Rhythmik und Metrik;* Hugo Leichtentritt, *Musikalische Formenlehre;* Abdy Williams, *The Rhythm of Modern Music;* Margaret H. Glyn, *Analysis of the Evolution of Musical Form.*

[2] *A critical study of traditional theory in the field of musica form,* George E. Conus (in Russian, not printed in translation), 1932.

Bücken's *Geist und Form;* but, for the most part, the terminology comes from prosody. Neither architectural nor poetic parallels represent music accurately; there are some advantages in the former when spans of attention need to be represented in modern music. But keeping in mind that idea-concepts differ radically from those of a spoken language, the devices of musical rhetoric can still be discussed in terms of sentences, thesis and antithesis, or even of rhyming parallels.

A typical illustration of the usual method is the following:

ILLUSTRATION Nº 11

W. A. MOZART
Piano Sonata

(*Illustration* No. 11). Here we have a musical statement complete in itself because its periodicity is established by the final full cadence (V-I), producing a punctuation akin to that of a period in a verbal sentence. This musical sentence is divided into two halves by another type of cadence, which for some reason is less conclusive in its effect than the final cadence. Because of its position at the middle of the sentence, this has been given the name 'half-cadence,' although this effect of colon or semi-colon, bifurcating the sentence, may be produced in different ways, some of which are not, strictly speaking, the 'half-cadence' of the harmony texts (x-V). In fact, most theorists admit even a full cadence at this point, if it is not as conclusive in its effect as the final full cadence, provided, for instance, some other note than the root of tonic or keynote is in the soprano. The first phrase may then be considered as the thesis of the sentence, to which the second phrase is antithesis, or answer. The effect of a sentence cannot be established, according to this theory, by a single phrase, whatever its length. There must be this division into answering phrases.

What do we mean by an answer in music? An answer implies relation to a question or statement that has been proposed. As we shall soon discover, relationships in modern music are extended to cover degrees of distance far removed from the obvious antithesis, a step higher, in Illustration No. 11. Provided the antithesis is recognized, the length of the sentence may vary, and the recognition of this variation is, to some extent, dependent upon tempo. At a slower tempo, four measures may be heard as a sentence, and at a faster tempo, sixteen, although eight may be considered the normal length. Let us take the first four measures of Illustration No. 12, and listen to them at an adagio tempo, in an attempt to discover whether the effect of a musical sentence is dependent upon relativity of tempo. The melodic outline might be represented in one letter for each measure (or 'section' of a possible four-measure sentence) as *ABCD*, and this would be considered by many a sufficient argument against a sentence of four measures here. After some experience with greater variety of melodic outline in more modern composers, other analysts would be able to point to parallel construction at locations slightly asymmetrical and with content greatly varied: for instance, the sixth g^2—b^1 of the first motive, answered by the sixth e^2—g^1 — with embellishment and passing-tones, to be sure — of motive three, or perhaps the rising melodic inflection of the first phrase, ending **d**—**d**-sharp—**e**, answered by the falling melodic inflection of the second phrase ending **a**—**g**. The more such parallels we hear, the more evidence we find for considering these four meas-

GUSTAV MAHLER
Fourth Symphony
First Subject

ILLUSTRATION № 12

ILLUSTRATION N⁰ 12 *(concluded)*

7 (extended)

8
(overlap with
1 of next sentence)

ures, when *adagio*, a four-measure sentence. Tempo itself, however, is an important feature of form, and should not be disregarded in any decision. Some attempts have been made to
measure spans of attention in psychological laboratories by time
units; but the reports differ so widely that the musician is forced
to disregard them and make a pragmatic decision. If asked the
question: "At the tempo of performance set by the composer, do
these first four measures constitute a sentence?" the answer is
'No'; and we shall find further justification for the answer when
we analyze the rest of the illustration, later, and discover that a
second sentence begins, like the first, at the end of the illustration,
by an overlap.

Returning to the Mozart illustration: each phrase is then
divided into two sections of two measures each, and each section

is analyzed as consisting of two motives of one measure each. None of these divisions were bounded by the bar-lines; in fact, they were all considered 'iambic,' as we shall see in Chapter V on the measure of the rhythm. However, their lengths total the combinations of $\frac{6}{8}$ measure, as stated. In a sentence of but four measures, the size of each feature is reduced by half, and similar adjustments must be made in regular sentences of other lengths. The phrase, then, is half of the sentence, the section is one-fourth, and the motive, one-eighth of the regular sentence. One must admit that the smaller divisions are often purely theoretical units; the divisions are not always present in the surface structure of the music itself. The term motive (not to be confused with the *leit-motif* of Wagner, which may be of any length) corresponds to the metrical measure of a 'foot' in poetry. It becomes a technical unit in scansion of music, and a division into 'feet' or motives in music may cut through the sense of the music just as an application of the parallel unit in poetry may divide a word: "The boy stood on the burning deck." '*ing-deck*' is the fourth foot of the line although it is not a unit of the sense. The fact that analysis into musical motives may do the same — unless we give up our foot-rule, or change its size from regular measure to ten or fourteen inches, as we please — is no valid objection to metrical analysis.

It cannot be denied, however, that the method of sentence analysis illustrated, as used by Riemann, Prout, and their followers, has been open to serious objections. They have limited the basic varieties of motives to but half the number used in poetic analysis, and they have then proceeded to analyze an art to which poets look in envy, hoping to imitate its larger freedom, with fewer 'measuring-rods' than the prosodists apply in the sister art. If we are to continue the analysis of sentence structure in modern music, we should not continue to limit motives to one classification, the iambic — a motive always beginning with an up-beat, or non-accent,—but should admit the possibility of trochaic varieties. Somewhat associated with this limitation of the older theory was the accusation that certain composers had misbarred their music. Riemann, for instance, re-edited music with 'corrections' based on this limited point of view. Others using the norm of eight measures with too great rigidity, demanded twice as many bar-lines, or in other cases, half as many.

Another criticism of the older theory concerns the process of bifurcating each structural feature, which made it impossible to call a sentence, consisting of two phrases, each of three measures, a regular six-measure sentence. Similarly, two equal phrases of five measures were denied regularity because the sections were two and three, or three and two measures, not two and one-half measures each. A more modern statement would admit regularity at one level in the structure and irregularity in a subdivision under that stratum. However, no stigma is attached to the word 'irregular' in modern music, and either point of view may be defended. The more serious question of limitation of analysis to iambic motives, with the resulting charge of misbarring, will be discussed more thoroughly in Chapter V.

Of course, many sentences were found which departed from the regular or normal type. The moderns have no monopoly upon irregularities in rhythmic structure; Bach's music presented the analysts with some of their most difficult 'mathematical' problems. They proceeded to reduce these irregularities to a basis of regularity, interpreting them in numbers representing departures from the regular order. If we wish to reproduce in outline all the possibilities, we need only state these in general terms, applicable to any object, including music: a regular continuum may be made irregular by changes at either end, or somewhere in the body of the object. These changes will make the object *larger* or *smaller* than the given norm. If *larger*, they may be produced by insertion of material; or, given a material capable of expansion, by stretching material already present to cover more space. If insertion is the method, this may be secured by repeated use of old material, or by the addition of new material.

If, on the other hand, the object is to be made *smaller*, or shorter, there are also three ways, and only three: elimination of some material; compression of the same material in a smaller space; or the overlapping of content.

This brief outline contains all the modifications which the analyst found and interpreted in a system of number-symbols. Illustration No. 12 may serve to introduce some of these, and, at the same time, represent one of the important forerunners of modernism, Gustav Mahler. It will be noticed that both the division into motives and the regularity of structure are more clearly indicated in the first part of the sentence. Usually this is the case; that is, a norm is established first, so that irregularities and the more continuous rhetoric of the latter part of the period may be more easily understood. The further we penetrate vertically into the smaller divisions of the theoretical structure, the less likely are we to find those divisions represented by breaks or commas in the musical expression; also, the farther we go horizontally in the sentence, the more continuous and yet the more irregular the construction usually becomes. This is not always the case. Sometimes the very outset of a sentence is irregular. In the Mahler sentence there are in reality three phrases, the third one extended to seven measures. Since these three stand in the relationship of one thesis to two antitheses, it is possible to reduce the whole to an eight-measure basis. The measures which are given two figures, 8-6, etc., have two relationships; in this case to what precedes, the measure is number 8, but some evasion of the final cadence is produced by insertion, and the relation to what follows is expressed in the second number. The last '7' is extended over two measures, and the final '8' overlaps with the entrance of melodic measure number 1 of a new sentence.

Thus far, we have merely illustrated methods of analysis used in the nineteenth century. Can we continue to use them in the music of the twentieth century? Throughout the entire course of sentences, much more irregular than the one just analyzed, the goal of the final cadence may still be recognized. We may enter many by-paths, or cut back upon our course, but we are not lost in this type of irregularity provided it has some reference to harmonic points of the compass. Can we retain the idea and effect of a musical period if the harmonic cadence disappears? Can we have eloquent irregularity and interesting side-excursions in the path of our musical thought without the orientation or sense of direction which this gave? Actually, the disappearance of the older harmonic-cadence has occurred in a process of such gradual modification that we have learned to find our way about without its help. If we divide the cadence into three parts represented in their simplest terms by IV-V-I, the history of harmony[1] has been one of increasing chromaticism, more elaborate structures representing these three steps, with added notes, elevenths and thirteenths, altered for greater dissonance. Chromatic modifications and superstructures of thirds do not of necessity change the progression of their roots. Both the sub-dominant, or precadence effect, and the dominant were altered and mixed in various proportions, until the cadence became a succession of non-tonic followed by some recognizable tonic. (In some of Schoenberg's *Sechs Kleine Stücke*, Opus 19, this results in six of the twelve notes followed by the other six.) The following Illustration (No. 13) from Milhaud's *Piano Sonata* (1916) shows a final tonic which is skillfully revealed by the erasure of non-tonic elements from a chord containing the entire tonic scale.

When the tonic itself received accretions of by-tones and a dissonant superstructure, only careful spacing or doubling still gave sufficient weight to the tonic elements for recognition as

---

[1] William Shield's *Harmony* presented the relationship of chords in a diagram not unlike an astronomical map. J. J. Virues y Spinola in his *Geneuphony* (1849) calls these three divisions "cadence, precadence, and transcadence." Casella's *Evolution of Music* is a modern treatment of the same subject. The writer's articles on *Harmony Reviewed* — the first of which was published in the February-March issue of the ***Music Educators Journal***, 1944, — generalize three classes of progressions, and point to an increase in directions away from a tonal center: V-ii-vi-iii in the first class, ii-IV-vi-I in the second, and vi-V-IV-iii-ii-I in the third. If there had been attraction or gravitation in the tonal solar system, it would appear that the musical universe was expanding, or some would say, disintegrating.

DARIUS MILHAUD
Piano Sonata (1916)
Final cadence

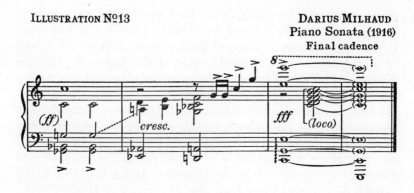

such.   Cadence then becomes again a problem of relativity
the final is relatively conclusive — a recognition which often
comes the moment *after* the composition has closed. This *was* a
final, we are able to say, because it presented more of the character of a close than what preceded. (*Illustration* No. 14, the
final cadence of Bartók's *Piano Suite IV*.)

Relativity may represent the difference between accents in
the rhythmic structure, or in melodic inflection, both of which will
be considered in other chapters. The gravitation of conflicting
lines into a unison, however, is in part melodic and in part harmonic. The overtones of a single note or octave come to the rescue
and supply harmonic resolution even when no other notes are
present. (The addition of a fifth without a third is even more
effective in Hindemith's cadences.) One is tempted to say that
some composers who write in an extremely dissonant style seem
to gravitate to finals in their compositions which use the octave C,
as if they were counting upon the connotation of many generations of use, for efficacy. Any attempt, however, to attach special
value to certain notes or chords as finals, is futile unless these
values have been established within the composition itself.
(*Illustration* No. 15.)

If successive phrases of dissonant material are all closed with
open octaves or fifths, the very absence of dissonance gives the

effect of punctuation. In an early example (*Illustration* No. 16),
the octave **B** brings the effect of a final tonic in spite of the fact

ILLUSTRATION №14

BÉLA BARTÓK
Piano Suite: Fourth Movement
Final ten measures

that the same **B** is also present in the preceding combination.
(In this case the chord **g,b,d,f** or **g, b, d, e**-sharp, the augmented

37

ERNST KRENEK (Op. 13)
Toccata and Chaconne
Final cadence

ILLUSTRATION № 15

CLAUDE DEBUSSY
Nocturnes I: *Nuages*
Final cadence

ILLUSTRATION № 16

sixth inside the dominant f-sharp takes the place of this dominant, and the cadence is secured in spite of the omission of this dominant and other notes of the tonic.) Provided some tonality has been established earlier in a composition, the final dissonant chord may be resolved to that tonic by the suggestion of the listener's imagination, without the addition of a single note of the tonic chord. (Schoenberg's Opus 19, No. 2. — *Illustration* No. 17.)

ARNOLD SCHOENBERG
From Opus 19, № 2
Last three measures
poco rit.

ILLUSTRATION № 17

A succession of periods that do not end with harmonic cadences results in what may be termed 'open construction,' as contrasted with the closed effect of sentences harmonically cadenced. It was early recognized that the development section of the sonata-form was constructed in this manner; and we find Wagner extending this continuous style until it covered almost an entire act, as one development. The arch of the form has become larger and larger until it now covers an entire movement or work; yet to ignore the presence of smaller units within this large construction, simply because the final cadences are absent, is to overlook many important details of the form. Continuity is secured by the avoidance of cadences, and the deceptive cadence becomes almost a mannerism of the Wagnerian style. It was the problem of form that bothered the contemporary audiences, and caused the accusation of 'endless melody.' Illustration No. 18 gives in abbreviation one feature of Wagner's form: we arrive at measure 8 to find it a half-way point to measure 16, but at measure 16, the music seems to be at the middle of a larger unit of

RICHARD WAGNER
'Parsifal'
Kundry's *Erzählung*

ILLUSTRATION No 18

(p)

10 measures omitted

measure 14

12 measures omitted

measure 15, cadence prepared for; full cadence avoided, as 16=half of 32

(etc.)

cadence again prepared   full cadence avoided

32 measures, and so on. This avoidance of *complete* finality—although the possible cadence points where the audience should 'come up for air,' seem obvious to-day—is an important stage on

the way to music in which cadence points are much less in evidence.

But little more advanced is a movement from one $^6_4$ chord, omitting the following dominant, to another $^6_4$, between which the music proceeds as from one pivot-point to another. (*Illustration* No. 19.) Schopenhauer asked for the satisfaction of the listener by a coincidence of rest and accent; but we have had more and more postponement of this satisfaction, with a lengthening of the suspense and a greater demand upon the tonal memory of each generation. We are finding satisfaction in a greater variety of harmonic interplay between these points; and the satisfaction, even if relative and not absolute, is all the greater because of this continual postponement. We learn to derive the satisfaction of cadence or resolution from effects which are not, in the old sense, final and complete.

One of the places to study the disappearance of the older punctuation of musical sentences is in the ten *Pianoforte Sonatas* of Scriabin. They represent a complete history of the change. Many pianists are familiar with the shorter works for piano, but too few are acquainted with the sonatas beyond the fourth. Composed in the years 1892–1913, these ten sonatas show how gradual were the changes in style. The first three have much that is derived from Schumann, Chopin, and Brahms. There is even that cross-reference of themes which we associate with César Franck's cyclical treatment. With the *Fourth Sonata* (1903) we note the transition to a more original harmonic style, although the cadence is still kept as punctuation throughout this work. In the *Fifth Sonata* (1908), we have, for the first time in this series, a sonata without a full cadence from beginning to end. And yet, as one listens to these sonatas in the order of composition, there is not much greater transition in style from the Fourth to the Fifth than from the Third to the Fourth. Musical sentences are still present, but the method of punctuation has changed.

An outline of the sentence-structure of the *Fifth Sonata* is

ILLUSTRATION №19

RICHARD STRAUSS
'Salome'

und das Ge-

heimnis der Lie - - - be ist gröss -

er als das Ge - heim - nis des To - des

(etc.)

given in the Appendix (I). At this point we will give in detail the
beginning of the exposition:[1] the first subject uses parallel con-

[1] Cf. also *The Piano Sonatas of Scriabin*, Karl Eschman, from *Proceedings* of
the Music Teachers National Association for 1934 (p. 57)

struction with homogeneous material (*Illustration* No. 20). Both the thesis and the antithesis are extended to six measures in repetitions of harmonies which are alike, but on different degrees. The next construction shows the same method of parallels. Note that the final '8' is repeated for weight or punc-

ILLUSTRATION N°20
Presto con allegrezza

ALEXANDER SCRIABIN (Op.53)
Fifth Sonata

tuation at this important point, just before the 'bridge' or transitional material begins, which moves toward the second subject. The bridge passage contains a new theme (*Illustration* No. 21), which illustrates in a simple way the same type of irregularity as in the older type of sentence, and may be easily understood as

ALEXANDER SCRIABIN
Fifth Sonata
Theme in 'bridge passage'

ILLUSTRATION №21 *(concluded)*

irregularity, when differentiation of material is as marked as here.

If there is no differentiation in harmonic material, established within the music itself, it is exceedingly difficult, if not impossible, to recognize periodic construction. If the differentiation remains, the material may be as dissonant as the composer desires, and sentences may still be determined. An increase in dissonance occurred in the Sixth and Seventh Sonatas of Scriabin, but the next illustration (*Illustration* No. 22) shows the opening of the Seventh as a regular 16 measure structure.

We may now attempt to re-define the musical sentence, changing the definition given by Prout (*Musical Form* — p. 7): "A passage ending with a full cadence, and which can be sub-divided by some form of middle cadence into at least two parts," to meet the conditions of analysis as we now find them:

A musical sentence is the statement of a musical idea which is relatively closed by a cadence produced by the repetition of harmonic weight, melodic inflection, and/or rhythmic generation, within which there is a structure of two parallel or related phrases, the first of which is closed by means less conclusive than those used to close the final phrase. (Melodic inflection and rhythmic generation will be discussed later.)

In the illustration just given, we have the same parallel structure in the first half of the sentence — even with the rhyming of measures 4 and 8 — that we have in the Mozart example (*Illustration* No. 11): at measure 8, however, the sentence swings forward to the second large division of the period, within which there is sufficient repetition of the final harmony to produce the effect of a full cadence, although it is only relatively closed in terms of the old definition. In this sentence, the repetition occurs *within* a rhythmic regularity. The repetition of dissonant combinations is similar in effect to the repetitions of the classical cadence V-I, V-I, etc.; the more important the point in the composition, the more repetition. These reiterations may later seem unnecessarily extended, as modern music, depending upon this method of cadence, becomes 'dated'; at the time they were

ILLUSTRATION № 22 *(concluded)*

written, it is as if the composer felt that he must give us enough of a particular combination so that we would agree with him that we had had enough, that the statement was 'closed' without doubt, and that we could go ahead with the next statement, or, if at the end, consider the whole matter closed.

There can be no question concerning the evidences of form in Scriabin's ten Sonatas. Some would say that they are too regular in form; and it is true that fours, eights, and sixteens occur frequently in his periods. It is an indication of the rapidity of changing musical vocabulary that we must consider him a conservative, but it is for this very reason that the logical form of the Sonatas furnishes a good introduction to the problems of modern music. Scriabin, by the way, should not be judged upon the basis of his orchestral works, nor upon the smaller piano pieces, such as his *Preludes*. He made certain contributions to the form of the sonata as a whole, which we will take up in a later chapter. Here we are more concerned with the disappearance of the harmonic-cadence as punctuation.

It is true that the new definition of a musical sentence places more responsibility upon individual decisions, concerning the inner content of the music, than the older definition, which asked for the recognition of definite 'ear-marks.' But is this not to be expected and welcomed? We do not wish to claim that this represents an 'advance,' as we are committed to changing historical standards. It is not a question of the superiority of the modern sentence. But at least the new sentence makes increasing demands upon the listener; he can not 'dream' through the periods to be comfortably reminded of the cadences when they arrive. It is as if our periods or 'stops' were omitted from our musical telegrams. We must depend upon the inner sense of the content to show us the integration.

Sentences, or periods, remain in modern music. The marks of punctuation have changed, but still may be recognized as based upon relative harmonic weight, provided this is established within the music itself, if it is not related in some way to a pre-established tonal hierarchy.

49

CHAPTER IV

PHRASE DETERMINATION
IN MELODIC INFLECTION

If we are to determine the phrase on the basis of melody, perhaps we should begin with the age-old question: What is melody? When a definition is attempted, however, we are forced back upon that 'vicious circle' of the psychologist: What the listener perceives as a melodic *Gestalt* is, for him, melody. Like the definition of electricity in science, it is a question of behavior, or the effect produced, rather than an exact description of its innermost mysteries. Let us begin, therefore, by performing an experiment.

In his book[1] on *Musical Form*, Ebenezer Prout wrote: "It is possible to write a succession of sounds which by no conceivable stretch of imagination can be called a melody, as, for example, the following:"

ILLUSTRATION №23   PROUT'S
                                                     Series

The reader is asked to test the validity of this statement by repeating the series of notes several times, returning to it again after the lapse of a few hours or days. As he continues to listen to these notes, in all probability he will find them changing into quite a satisfying melody, and one which is certainly less radical than the following melody of Anton von Webern:

[1] Prout, *Musical Form* (p. 2), 1893.

50

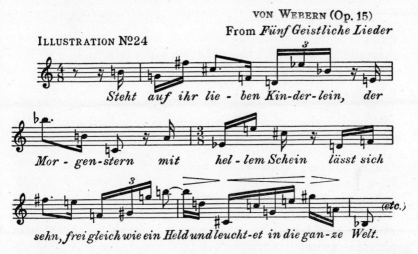

ILLUSTRATION №24

von Webern (Op. 15)
From *Fünf Geistliche Lieder*

Steht auf ihr lie - ben Kin-der-lein, der

Mor - gen-stern mit hel - lem Schein lässt sich

sehn, frei gleich wie ein Held und leucht-et in die gan-ze Welt.

The contrast between Prout's statement and the Webern art-song is but another illustration of the distance travelled in the last fifty years. Of course, what we have been doing in our experiment is to discover, or, some would say, read into the Prout series, the inflections of form; that is, we hear the series as a sentence. It may be interesting to follow the steps through which Prout, in 1893, proceeded to write a melody for his book. First, he places all the notes in the same tonality, but without ending on the tonic. Finding this still unsatisfactory, Prout next ends on the tonic, but places the middle cæsura, or cadence, left of center. He objects to this asymmetrical division, and finally produces a conventionally regular sentence. At *some* point in the argument, many listeners, to-day, would desert his side. We may prefer Prout's asymmetrical sentence to his neatly regular one, possibly because of its more interesting rhetorical structure.[1]

[1] A parallel illustration may be found in the problem of harmonic resolution and relative 'consonance' as presented in the original first edition of the *Seashore Talent Tests*. The tests on Consonance and Melodic Taste have been withdrawn from the revised edition of these tests. Why? I do not know that it has been clearly acknowledged, or sufficiently emphasized, that the revision was made because so many of the best musicians and students tested, consistently preferred the 'bad' but more suggestive and interesting combinations.

51

16844

For those who still stand with Prout in maintaining that his series of notes is an impossible melody, a re-reading of the series may add the force of form, and serve as an introduction to the subject of modern melody:

ILLUSTRATION №25

Iambic motives, symmetrical sections and phrase punctuation have produced a melodic sentence that has some attractive features in which a modernist might find possibilities of beauty, if treated as a subject of a *chaconne*. The theorist with a modern attitude might analyze it, in academic fashion. The second phrase is, as usual, continuous, and the modal cadence, **f-g**, brings the sentence to a satisfactory end. The beginning is clearly a melodic decoration of the dominant harmony; by the use of enharmonic spelling: **a**-flat for **g**-sharp, Neapolitan decoration for the **g′** characteristic of Schoenbergian dispersed harmony, and with the borrowing of **e**-flat or **e**-natural in a modern major-minor scale, the melody is not impossible even from a theoretical standpoint. In addition, an impious fate seems to have forced Prout to place the highest note three-fourths of the way through, at the best point for a climax, the point at which it occurs in classical drama as well as in the Webern melody already cited.

Turning again to Webern, Prout seems at first quite regular by comparison. But as we also become familiar with the melody of this art-song, we discover melodic inflection, rhyming the two phrases. There is also some agreement in the sectional structure at "Kinderlein" and "hellem Schein." The setting of the words, as we expect in an art-song, is admirable: the natural inflection which a speaker would use for "ihr lieben Kinderlein" is followed, and the wide range that is used for these words may be justified on extra-musical grounds in imitation of the larger inflections of emotional speech. The 'whole musical world' of the singer is appropriately used on the words "ganze Welt." The rhyming of "Morgenstern" with "ganze Welt" is asymmetrical, but the entire melody is an excellent example of variety — unified in modern idiom. The final note is the lowest of all, and there can be no question about the feeling of cadence produced.

If this experiment has been conducted successfully, and all of the implications of the Prout series and the Webern melody are understood, the result is a pragmatic definition of melody.

Musical articulation, which was formerly so clearly punctuated by a combination of harmonic, melodic, and rhythmic means that coincided in effect and in complete agreement, may now depend in a given work upon one type of punctuation at a time. Cæsuras in the past have been indicated by melodic inflection and by harmonic cadence as well as rhythmic discharge; we must now depend in some cases upon one of these alone with but slight assistance from the other two. In the preceding chapter we considered methods of indicating periodicity by the relative weight of tonal combinations used for cadences. Some of them we can scarcely call harmonies, for they may not involve harmonic relationships in the old sense. A style based exclusively upon repetitions of homogeneous material in parallel vertical combinations, however, could become unbearably monotonous without at least a little 'pointing' to relieve the monotony; so the possibility of melodic inflection, which is considered in this chapter, is never entirely absent, and is particularly useful in the determination of the phrase as a unit. In the chapter that follows this, rhythmic self-generation, on the basis of the still smaller units, will complete this division of the subject.

All three facets of musical appearances: the harmony, the melody, and the rhythm, are so related in a sort of 'trinitarian' unity that it is impossible to discuss one without some reference to the other two. For instance, the suspension as a melodic inflection may become a landmark having harmonic foundation even when preparation, suspension, and resolution are all dissonant. But a noticeable trend away from the harmonic foundations of melodic and contrapuntal technique cannot be denied. This is one reason why Hindemith's *Wir bauen eine Stadt* sounds more like the fourteenth century than like the eighteenth. In his second volume of the *Unterweisung*,[1] which is devoted to the teaching of melodic writing in one and two parts, the implication of underlying harmonies is avoided in every possible way by rule and by example; this is in contrast with the nineteenth century texts on counterpoint, which discuss and demand a clearly understood harmonic procedure. There are other elements in Hindemith's style, among them the return to *organum* in part, parallel sevenths in a modern version of de Machault, the increased importance of the fourth as a vertical consonance, which aid in producing neo-primitive effects; but no one feature is more important than the inflection of his melodies and their studied avoidance of harmonic implications. Broken chords are not permitted: "If in spite of insertion (of intervening notes) the ear hears the tonal grouping as a retardation of the melodic flow, the grouping should be given up."[2]

We are associating melodic inflection with the phrase, not because it is absent at other points in the structure, but because, as we have seen in the last chapter, with the weakening of the harmonic cadence, the melodic inflection becomes more important in determining the phrase. The need for taking a breath — whether physical or mental — in performance and in listening, retains the phrase as a structural element even when the pairing as thesis and antithesis, with the half-cadence of the former rhyming with the full cadence of the latter, has lost much of its obviousness with the increasing loss of definiteness in the sentence itself.

We have seen that it is necessary to accept the idea of relativity: the musical thought is left relatively 'open' or is relatively 'closed' at certain points of punctuation; the modern phrase presents a musical idea which is less definitely closed than is the

[1] *Craft of Musical Composition*, New York: **Associated Music Publishers,** 1941.
[2] *Unterweisung* (Vol. II, p. 7).

larger division, the period, of which it is a part. On the other hand it is more 'closed' at its limits, its beginning and its end, than at any point within these limits. If this idea of relative finality as the sole distinction between the end of a period and the end of a phrase seems lacking in definiteness, so is the music to which it applies.[1]

With a flexible definition (which the conservative may criticize as no definition at all), the term 'phrase' is retained in this discussion. Unfortunately, printed directions for performance cannot be depended upon to indicate the phrase analysis of form. The curved line is used for so many different purposes; even when used systematically, it may present the ideas of an editor, using a stereotyped system, such as Riemann's; often it is used without reference to formal units, covering the contents of varying numbers of measures with lines of legato, neatly ending at bar-lines. We cannot depend upon printed commas; in our reading or performance their location will be dictated by the content of the music. The melodic contour influences the decision, as is indicated by the original meaning of the word 'cadence,' 'to fall,' in approaching the final. Psychologists are not agreed as to the reason for our association of 'high' and 'low' with notes of relative pitch,[2] and the Greek system seems to avoid any reference to a law of gravitation by reversing the theoretical order. However, most primitive music uses melodic inflection, phrases beginning high in the Amerindian singer's range, for instance, and then

[1] Reichenbach's *Formenlehre* (p. 48) states that the Psalmodies, or Gregorian patterns for each mode, divide into two phrases, the end of the first of which is recognized as "a rest upon the way, after which the journey is continued with redoubled strength." His graphs present the appearance of a mountain to be climbed:

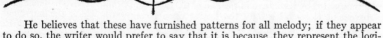

He believes that these have furnished patterns for all melody; if they appear to do so, the writer would prefer to say that it is because they represent the logical trajectory of thought, or, in terms of Bergson, the history of organism in general: *élan, épanouissement et chute,*" and that it is this fundamental logic which has produced the Psalmodies as well as present-day melodies.

[2] C. C. Pratt, in *The Meaning of Music*, believes that he has established that "phenomenologically, tones do have higher or lower locations in space."[2]

descending in varying tonal contours to lower and lower levels like a stream of melody. If the lowest level is the same for most phrases of the same melody, it comes to have the force of a tonic; but this method of phrase cadence can be used as in the Webern melody, without the repetition of the *same* low point. Herbert Bedford, an English composer of modern unaccompanied song, has presented similar treatment in his *If Music be the Food of Love.* The law of gravitation in music being satisfied, a new energy seems to lift the range only to start again a new descent. In the solo sonatas of Hindemith, there is much more artistic development of the rising phrase, but in the end "what goes up, generally comes down," and this may be due to the fact that the lower the note, the more weight the overtones of that note are able to add to the finality effect of harmonic-partials.[1]

In this alternation of potential storage and discharge there is propulsion and form. Melodic inflection is used not merely in unaccompanied melody. If that were the case, it would deserve only limited consideration. It is effective in homophonic and complicated contrapuntal music, alike. (In the *Suite for Piano* by Richard Donovan (*New Music*, April, 1933), polytonal, if not atonal, music comes to rest at the end of each of the four movements on the notes **e, f, e-b,** and **c**-sharp, respectively.) There is, of course, no question that this occurrence of potential storage and discharge was true of tonal music in which the melodic inflection decorated and reinforced the harmonic inflection. With tonality, certain tendencies are set up in tones, and the movement tends to be like that of electricity over the shorter gaps. Perhaps

[1] When writing for a solo string instrument, Hindemith frequently uses the method of closing on the lowest open string. For instance, in *Sonata for Viola* (solo), Op. 11, No. 5, the First, Second, and Fourth Movements close on the low **C** (accompanied by its octave in the end of the first and last movements). The Second Movement closes with only the lowest open string, with which the movement began. Its use is saved for important points in the form of the movement: after two low **C**'s at measures 1 and 6, it appears but once at a cadence, measure 25, and then as final 'pedal' seven times in the last eight measures. The Third Movement, which is the only one not ending with the lowest **C**, ends with the lowest **C**-sharp.

One movement of his *Sonata for Violin* (solo) ends with the reiteration of **c′, b, a, g** (lowest note on the instrument) eleven times.

the absence of such pulls as that of the leading-tone, by half-step
to the tonic, accounts for so many wide skips in atonal music,
where the electrical current of tonality is not present, but where

ILLUSTRATION No. 26

ALEXANDER SCRIABIN
Seventh Sonata

Avec une volupté radieuse

a musical law of gravitation still seems to operate, as in the
Webern melody.

The effect of melodic inflection, as well as of the new 'harmonic
cadences' of the preceding chapter, is geometrically strengthened
by repetition. The trill (*Illustration* No. 26), grace-note, or any
feature of melodic decoration, is sufficient to call attention to

57

punctuation if repeated. What the poet calls phonetic 'syzygy' guarantees their acceptance. Certain other mechanical divisions can be set up, not only by rests of longer or shorter length, but by contrast subordinated to the phrase content. When strummed accompaniment was used by early bards, the cæsuras of the vocal-line were filled with instrumental 'chords,' long before chords were related to implied tonalities. Just the reverse of this method was consciously used by Herbert Howells in his suite, *In Green Ways* (as indicated in a conversation with the composer), where bits of recitative are used to indicate cæsuras in successions of chord masses.

While final and more important inflections are usually in the downward direction, there are often less final and less important intermediate cæsuras in which the melodic inflection is upward. (The harmonic half-cadence is often considered 'above' the old harmonic final cadence.) These intermediate inflections remind one of the directions for singing the prose scriptures: "Thus sing the comma, and thus the colon, and thus the full stop." (*Illustra-*

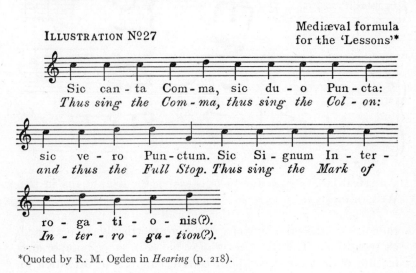

ILLUSTRATION №27

Mediæval formula
for the 'Lessons'*

Sic can - ta Com - ma, sic du - o Pun - cta:
Thus sing the Com - ma, thus sing the Col - on:

sic ve - ro Pun - ctum. Sic Si - gnum In - ter -
and thus the Full Stop. Thus sing the Mark of

ro - ga - ti - o - nis(?).
In - ter - ro - ga - tion(?).

*Quoted by R. M. Ogden in *Hearing* (p. 218).

tion No. 27.) A wide leap in the melodic outline necessarily carries with it increased attention, and this heightened attention is, properly speaking, a type of accent, quite apart from dynamic considerations.

These inflections in tonal music upon a harmonic basis were adapted, as the name implies, to the 'sense' of the musical idea in the way that inflections of the speaking voice may be expected to agree with the ideas expressed. Our difficulty begins when we try to use inflection as the main basis of analysis. A greater burden is placed upon the perception and retention of pattern in melodic phrases. At the same time, since these patterns seem to be not entirely divorced from a musical law of gravitation, this is not so difficult as the recognition of the Schoenbergian Series (cf. Chapter VI) 'in a vacuum' without their operation.

The length of a melodic phrase may vary within rather wide limits. There has been some attempt to study the span of attention in psychology, but the limit to perception without grouping (that is, closing the span) has been given such a wide range, .01 to 2.0 minutes,[1] that there is little help at this point for the analysis of music. Doubtless it varies with individuals, and certainly it is not independent of relative complexity of content in the span. In this connection there have been two main criticisms of modern music, from Wagner on: one, that 'the melody is endless,' and the other, that music has lost the 'long breath' or wide sweep of melody, and is too fragmentary. If there are no units or divisions in structure either above or below the phrase, then we can recognize the validity of both of these criticisms, although they may, at first glance, seem somewhat contradictory.

Analysis which recognizes only phrases as spans of attention needs to discover some basis for organization of these phrases into other strata. In listening to a 'Concerto for two player-pianos,' which may be written without any regard for performers' limitations, the hearer will either subdivide the music or close his

---

[1] Reported in MacEwen: *The Thought in Music.*

ears. Try as he may, then, he will not be able to give equal emphasis, equal attention to each and all of these subdivisions. A kind of emergent evolution forms larger entities which, for want of other terminology, we might as well call 'periods' or 'sentences.' If repetition in parallels has a tendency to pall, as it does in some music of French impressionism, then asymmetry can be used. When attention is concentrated upon a single melodic line, or when that line is accompanied in modern homophonic style, connections may be established over greater distances, and a greater degree of irregularity is possible in the size of phrases. Melodic decoration or inflection makes asymmetry possible, and if the Western mind indicates in the twentieth century a preference for this, it may be evidence of the completion of a historical cycle, or an increased appreciation of oriental music.

Erwin Stein[1] believes it is improbable that any coördinating principle may develop from the theory of harmony (such as we attempted to suggest in the last chapter). Rather, he expects it to arise from melodic theory. It is true that the Schoenbergian Series may be used with due regard to the 'phrase.' When used with great freedom in relation to the rhythmic form, they present certain difficulties, to be discussed later; however, there is an increased emphasis upon the horizontal point of view and melodic cogency, which is all the more important as the harmonic structure dissolves. Just as the need for a *cantus firmus* was felt before the rise of harmonic autocracy, so we need and we discover in some modern music, if not a fixed or firm song, at least certain evidences of melodic integration.

The smaller units we may leave to subconscious reception, or a kind of metronomic instinct. We listen more 'by phrases.' Even when the 'phrases' are constructed from measures of different sizes, the fact may not attract the attention of a listener; as we shall see in the next chapter, phrases so constructed out of 'odd and ends' of measure sizes, often reach the same totals. The

[1] *Von Neuer Musik* (p. 59).

phrase is an extremely important division of modern form, and in the phrase, melodic inflection is of prime importance; but this is not the same as saying that it is the only recognizable unit, or that harmonic and rhythmic considerations may now be disregarded. In analysis of the phrase, melodic inflection is usually the determining factor, and absolute levels of pitch may be effective when relative levels based upon harmonic tendencies are not obviously present in the music.

CHAPTER V

THE MEASURE OF THE RHYTHM

The literature on Rhythm is voluminous. In a temporal art, the entire study of morphological structure is a study of rhythm, the rhythm of the whole and of its smallest particle. As we approach a consideration of the unit of measurement, which has been given the term 'motive,' we again face the problem of definition. A definition in terms of subdivision, "one-eighth of the regular sentence," is not entirely satisfactory in these days, when the lengths of sentences are difficult to determine.

If we begin by asking how motives arise and how they behave, we may secure evidences of form that will be useful in analysis, although a final or conclusive definition eludes us. A series of exact and equal beats, represented by notes uniform in all respects, may be produced scientifically, but they are not heard as such. We add a subjective accent not present in actual fact, which groups the notes of that series about accents, and these accents represent the nuclei of rhythmic motives. These motives then seem to combine into larger groups in what might be termed a self-generating rhythm, provided we remember, when we use that term, that it represents not a materialistic but rather a psychologically constructivistic process.

Fascinating fields for speculative digression tempt us at this point: the mysteries of numbers and their generative forces; philosophical problems of matter and mind; percept and concept, as well as the emphasis of modern science upon the primal character of rhythm in vibration. Recent theories of the origin of music have given rhythm the place of greatest importance, and highly organized music in its most elaborate forms owes its ability to parallel the dynamics of emotion, in large measure, to *motion* as the stem of emotion. Rhythmic form in the largest aspects of musical architecture, as well as in its smallest details, has an emotional appeal as its result, and, in all probability, as its cause. This should not be forgotten by those who minimize the importance of form as purely 'intellectual.'

Avoiding the questions: "Does Rhythm generate Melody?" and "Does Accent raise Pitch?" which a rhythmic theory of origins seems to raise, and which remind us of the question: "Does Matter generate Mind?", we reach the more practical but still difficult questions: Is there a rhythmical unit of 'one?' Are 'twos' and 'threes' the only primary units? If we extend the motive-unit on the basis of non-divisibility into other like units, **101** and an unending series of prime numbers could be included theoretically, as well as the **5**'s, **7**'s, or **11**'s, which we may wish **to** include practically. If 'five' is included as an 'asymmetrical compound,' is this always either **2** and **3** or **3** and **2**,— or may it also be **2** and **2** and **1**, **1** and **2** and **2**, or **2** and **1** and **2**? An answer to this last question is dependent, of course, upon our answer to the first of these practical questions. This may be sufficient to indicate the puzzling problems we meet when we attempt to examine the rhythmic process microscopically.

The nucleus of accent — which we have thus far considered in its simplest form as a psychological or subjective emphasis non-existent in the material, so far as scientific determination is concerned — presents its own group of questions when we begin to embody it in musical form. Accent is produced by any method which sets off an item of material for special attention. There are dynamic accents of stress, and agogic accents of length. Any organist knows that the latter seem to produce the former. There is the accent produced by the lowest item in pitch, and the accent produced by the highest item. In the latter there is a potential force, and in the former the weight of discharge of this force in musical gravitation. There may be superimposed upon these, or substituted for them, many other kinds of accent, (*a*) color or tone quality, (*b*) relative value in a pre-established harmonic hierarchy, as well as (*c*) the relative importance which mere

63

repetition gives in attracting attention to tonal items. Any attempt to organize all of these in the order of relative importance would compel us to begin each statement with the phrase: "Other things being equal;" for this smallest unit of the structure is so complex in character, subject to so many influences and interpretations, that, again, any definition of the secret of musical life has eluded us. We can only describe the appearance and behavior of organisms — *not* explain them.

To adopt a modern point of view, we should be ready to admit the possibility of motives of one or any number of beats, and, at the same time, we must accept the conclusions of the psychologist — confirmed by common sense observation of our own musical behavior, — that numbers which offer the *possibility* of division into multiples of smaller units have a strong tendency to divide. Numbers not so divisible also tend to break up into subdivisions, even if only asymmetrical fracture is possible. Furthermore, common sense tells us that the number **one** is not intelligible as a rhythmic unit by and of itself. It must either relate itself to another, or it must subdivide itself to reproduce. In **5** as **2** and **2** and **1** we understand the final **one**, only in relation to the **2** and **2** preceding, as a remainder-fraction, or, more logically, as an asymmetrical division of a final **three**, that is, **5** equals **2** and **3** (subdivided **2** and **1**). To conclude this paragraph, which attempts to summarize a compromise position of 'common sense' in these answers, it should be pointed out that classical composers were able to get rhythmic subtlety in subdivisions within the regularity of bar-lines. Much of their music, if written to-day, might be presented by measures of varying sizes. On the other hand, much modern music could be returned to a regular measure, provided phrasing, connecting balkens, accent, and punctuation marks preserve the integration.

In the chapter on the Phrase, we stated that lengths of phrases were often approximately equal, even if the measured subdivisions changed. This is often true of Cyril Scott's music, which looks much more irregular than it sounds. "The Twilight of the Year"

(Number four of the 'Poems') answers four measures of $\frac{5}{8}$ by two of $\frac{3}{4}$ and one of $\frac{4}{4}$, but the total in each phrase is *twenty* eighths. An interesting experiment was performed by Dr. Patterson of the Department of English, Columbia University, which gives a possible parallel in modern poetry. Amy Lowell was asked to read the following lines[1] for a phonograph record:

> There was a man
> Who made his living
> By painting roses
> Upon silk.
> He thought only of roses
> And silk.
>
> When he could get no more silk
> He stopped painting
> And only thought
> Of roses.

The distances between the primary accents were then measured, and the time was found to be approximately the same, regardless of the length of the line or the number of syllables between accents. In some respects, modern music is like 'free verse' in its demand for a greater variety in the length of the unit-measure. As long as this variety does not disturb the structure at higher levels, the music is felt as innocuously regular by many listeners.

It is only when the more complicated units of number are extended to the higher levels that the composer's structure presents a more involved style; that is, we have binary and ternary primary forms, but can we have quintuple successions of new material at that level? This presents a problem to be discussed in a later chapter.

The modern practice, then, is to change time-signatures where, formerly, the content-accent, or what might be called the 'agogic' or even the 'vowel' accent, was felt as a very subtle *rhythmic counterpoint*, or syncopation, against the regular barring.

[1] From the poem: "A Painter of Silk," by Amy Lowell. *Used with the permission of* Houghton Mifflin Company, Boston.

Which is the better plan? Each has its advantages and disadvantages, and there is no good reason to pit one against the other. Hans Pfitzner (in *Musikalische Impotenz*) criticized Alban Berg for his intricacy, but left himself open to attack when he referred to Schumann's *Träumerei* as a "simple melody for piano, 2 hands"; for Berg (in *The New Æsthetic of Hans Pfitzner*) shows how extremely intricate is the motive structure of the *Träumerei*, and how it might well be written in measures of varying sizes.[1]

Whatever the size of the motive, the latter is recognized upon its repetition, and the two motives form a duple synthesis at the next higher level in the structure. Once set up, the unit remains in force until some feature of content forces us to change; even then there is a strong prejudice — a *pre-judgment* in favor of the old, and syncopations may be maintained for some time without disturbance. There is a temptation to think of musical motives as time-units empty of content. This is possible, but only after the unit has been set up in and *through* content. After that, one sound may be extended over the space of time ordinarily occupied by two or more units, or we may find the place of the unit occupied by a 'rest.' The final measures: 𝄞 or: 𝄞 which Beethoven uses at the end of no less than ten movements of his Pianoforte Sonatas are interesting illustrations of the composer's sensitiveness to temporal proportions. Two of these come at the end of the complete sonatas, so that the rest is not terminated by further sound, that is, not even by the beginning of another movement. They may seem unnecessary, but they are found to be required for the completion of the formal unit analyzed. Another illustration of the same sensitiveness is seen in number four, Andante from Bartók's *Für Kinder* (*Illustration No. 28*). Here, there are just sixteen measures, including the final measure of rest; but it would appear that this is measure eight, which is omitted at the middle, but which is found at the

[1] For another study of the same, cf. Walter Goldstein, *Rhythmic Tricks*, from *Proceedings* of the Music Teachers National Association for 1924 (p. 63).

end as a measure of rest concluding the entire piece. Bartók marks his division by a short vertical line through the fourth and fifth line of the treble-clef.

ILLUSTRATION №28

BÉLA BARTÓK
From *Für Kinder,* № 4

Andante

Mensuration is a fairly recent development, as we know from the history of music. Much was performed and written before this measuring process was set up, and there seems to be a strong movement against the 'tyranny of the bar-line' among modern composers. The bar-line may continue to be used in some cases as a visual aid for combined performance, without the implication that the beat which follows the bar-line has any special accent. At present, the measure is used in varying ways: the standard may change at almost every bar (in some cases, 'without notice');[1] the measure may be of such length as to amount to phrases or sentences, or the bar-lines may be entirely omitted. An early example of the last, written in 1894, is the *Prélude de la Porte Héroique du ciel*, by Erik Satie; but, for this, imaginary bar-lines may easily be supplied by reading the content. We marvel at the ability of sixteenth century singers to perform without the aid of bar-lines; and that ability could be developed again; but it is unlikely that the bar-line will entirely disappear except, perhaps, in solo works for one performer, or for one performer and subordinate accompaniment.

When the measures reach inordinate length, bar-lines might as well be omitted, so far as the determination of the musical 'foot' is concerned, although they may help in the larger divisions. Hába, in his *Fantasie* (Opus 9a) for violin solo in quarter-tones, has, in all, fifty-seven measures; but of these about one-third have the value of from ten to thirty-five quarter-notes each. Obviously, in measures of this size, when the material is not of cadenza character, the bar-line cannot perform the entire accenting function. The last eight measures contain the equivalent of 145 quarter-notes in the order: 10, 8, 20, 10½, 28½, 18, 15, and 35. In this case, it is obvious that the performer must depend upon something other than bar-lines. Balkens become important: that is, when the notes are all of the same denomination, the integration can be indicated by the connection of the stems of the notes to a balken; but this can be used only if the notes are short enough in value to have 'flags' (hooks).

---

[1] The writer can see no reason for this in Busoni's *Second Sonata* for piano, or in many works of Hindemith. When it does not bother the reader, it may serve the purpose of avoiding the *appearance* of a new formal division, which used to accompany a time-change; but anyone acquainted with modern music knows the relative unimportance of time-changes in the large form. Hindemith has a still more confusing practice of setting up a time-signature, changing to another, and expecting the performer to revert to the first, without notice; in some cases in the next measure. If this marking of 'exceptions' is used, *each* exceptional measure should be marked, or the return should be indicated.

ALOIS HÁBA (Op. 9ª)
Fantasie for Violin Solo
Eleventh measure

ILLUSTRATION № 29

In the above: ↳ raises the note a quarter-tone,

ↆ lowers the note a quarter-tone,

♯↲ raises the note three-fourths of a tone.

In this 'measure' of Hába's, there are seventeen repetitions of a group of six eighth-notes. Superimposed upon this integration are the printed curves of the bowing, which bring out other repeated patterns in the unbroken succession of eighth-notes.

If a composer is to use different indications of punctuation, there is some need for a statement of the order of importance which he attaches to the various signs when that is not self-evident. For instance, in this same composition, which consists of four movements, the first movement uses the bar-line sixteen times in a total of 462½ quarter-notes. The largest measure contains 62 quarters. The sign **//**, placed on the top line of the staff, seems to indicate a larger break in the structure than the bar-line, since it occurs but ten times. However, the last four of these signs (**//**) occur *within* the final measure of 52½ quarters, which would make the sign appear as a subordinate division of the measure. (The first six signs do coincide with bar-lines.) The second movement dispenses with bars entirely and uses the sign (**//**) twice, dividing the movement into three parts, of which the last one, in size, and to a certain extent in content, balances the first. Here, the sign outlines the *large* form. The third movement uses no bar-lines, but adds a new sign borrowed from its early use in Gregorian notation, a heavy, short, vertical line through the top line of the staff, as well as double slanting lines **//**. The division is as follows:

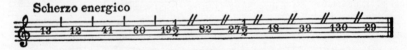

Scherzo energico

The figures refer to the time-interval between the respective marks, reduced to their value in quarter-notes. There is no indication of any change in tempo, and no mark of expression related to time, although there are a number related to dynamics. It would appear from the above that the 'Gregorian' vertical line was used for less important divisions in the initial statement of the idea.

The fourth movement (Moderato risoluto) uses but one bar-line, and has none of the other indications above; but in this movement the variety and pattern of content may be used by the performer as a basis for his interpretation; and other indications are not as necessary here as they are in the Scherzo, where all but four of the first 257 notes are quarter-notes!

Enough has been said to indicate that we have a right to expect — before the end of the twentieth century, at least — some new punctuation *marks* in our music, as in our written prose, for which relative values can be accepted. Whether these will take the form of:

   a) bar-lines, dotted and solid, single and double, light or heavy;

   b) the use of period (.), comma (,), semi-colon (;) and colon (:), etc. — borrowed from language;

   c) marks for accented and non-accented syllables — from poetry.

or some new hierarchy, cannot be foretold. All of the above have been tried. Schoenberg uses the signs for accent and nonaccent, ' and ˘, in his *Suite für Klavier* (Opus 25), (cf. *Illustration* No. 6 of Chapter II); but here he uses them to indicate a relationship *within* a measure in the *Præludium* (where they occur but once in measure 22); and also in the *Gigue* (where they occur frequently). .They are contradictions of the natural accents.

The music of Stravinsky, especially of his earlier period, notably *Le Sacre*, illustrates the synthetic constructive force of rhythm, which is itself creative,— generating and thus explaining its own content. This is to be expected as a prominent feature of music for modern ballets; and since it is also found in the rhythms of machinery, we find the two may combine in a *Ballet mechanique*. While the music is measured by gradations of accent, differences of content also create accents; although the parallel is not exact, we may think of the older harmonic values as the equivalent of qualitative distinctions in the vowel sounds of classic verse, which are replaced to a considerable extent by quantity, or accent, in such composers as Stravinsky and Bartók.

The natural tendency of equal sounds, in repetition, to form patterns, cannot be relied upon to form an *artistic* pattern. Rather, if we follow the natural line of least resistance, this leads to a monotonous repetition of the simplest arrangement. A familiar instance is the noise of the railway car on the rails. An artistic pattern with some irregularity must be indicated by a notation and dictated by the composer; for art is essentially *super*-natural, that is, superimposed upon the natural, and requires a dictation of form. It is <u>arti</u>ficial, and if we emphasize the first syllable of that word we may change the connotation which it has received in a century that followed Rousseau 'back to nature.' Without question, a duple division is superimposed more readily than a triple unit, and the primacy of the dual division cannot be denied at higher levels as well. This does not mean that **8** must always consist of four times two; **3** and **3** and **2**, **2** and **3** and **3**, or **3** and **2** and **3** are all different and more interesting, especially when treated as **5** and **3** or **3** and **5** in what might be called asymmetrical duple divisions. These appear in divisions of measures of Ravel's *String Trio* and Debussy's *Sonata II* for Flute, Viola, and Harp. If we insist that the dotted measures are the units in these cases, we see how rhythm alone can produce intricate forms of sections and phrases, as well. European music that has some slight contact with folk-song influenced by Asiatic music, furnishes many illustrations. Many of Bartók's smaller pieces are based upon **3** and **2** and **3** with repetitions, **6** and **4** and **6**; and in larger units this becomes the structure of the second theme of his Piano Sonata.

As a matter of fact, whatever the size of the rhythmic unit, the problem is the same. It is added evidence of the integrity of this art, to-day, as always, that as microsm or as macrosm the same features are present and the same relationships may be established. While it would simplify our problem to say that each succession of two or three sounds forms a musical unit, or 'foot-motive,' the rapidity with which these sounds occur has such a bearing upon the degree to which we see or hear the music microscopically, as to make this procedure unprofitable. Whatever unit we take we are in the predicament of the physicist or chemist who decides upon an atom as his unit, only to find, later, that instead of being an irreducible unit, the atom is a universe in itself.

The unit we select depends upon two features: (1) the determination of an accent or nucleus, and (2) the determination of the size of the unit measure, *i.e.*, the distance between this accent and the next one of comparable importance. When these two are recognized, there still remains, for the theorist, the location of the nucleus within the motive. With two sounds there is the choice of what we may call iambic ′ or trochaic ′ ⌣ order. Hugo Riemann gives us no choice in the matter, but analyzes all music as iambic. The application of this theory of scansion results in the charge of mis-barring, from which not even the greatest composers have escaped. Stewart Macpherson — one of Riemann's followers — refers[1] to "those cases, *unfortunately* not infrequent, where the composer has *inadvertently* barred his music *inaccurately*" (Italics added). When we place the bar-lines where he wants them in Schubert's *Impromptu* (Opus 142), B-flat-major, we find that we lose the composer's fine rhythmic play of 'counterpoint' in adjustment between a quality-or-harmonic accent and a quantity-or-dynamic accent. It would be just as absurd a limitation to say that all motives are trochaic, although Hermann Keller[2] believes that he has discovered the basis for historical preferences. He states that the trochaic arrangement was very widely used at the time of Bach, and that it maintained this position until about the time of Beethoven, even during a period of considerable uncertainty, when articulation was often confused with the indications for bowing, etc. Keller considers the trochaic order appropriate for the classical period, while the iambic order, with its crescendo of interest to an accent, is more favored in a romantic and more dramatic period. One might add, as a further influence, the rise of the conductor; he must prepare for an attack even when there is no music in the up-beat, and so he suggests an iambic arrangement. One might even say that conductors are required in a romantic period, but are less necessary in neatly classical performances. The best performances of small groups of

[1] In *Form and Music* (p. 39).
[2] In *Die Musikalische Artikulation.*   Stuttgart: Schultheiss, 1925.

old instruments are those in which conducting, if done, is as inconspicuous as possible.

Perhaps the solution that allows for the greatest freedom and subtlety is found in a relationship at all times in both directions, just as in harmony there is a vertical and horizontal attraction. If there is a predilection during a classical period for the trochaic, and in a romantic period for the iambic, it is well to remember both possibilities, especially the one in lesser use. Perhaps it was the carrying over of classical indications into a romantic period which Riemann felt should be 'corrected.' At the opening of this century we feel that Riemann, in turn, needs correction, and in all cases we need to have a wholesome respect for the original manuscript indicating the composer's point of view. The iambic movement was a reaction from those editions in which all phrase marks ended at the bar-lines; but to make everything iambic goes to the other extreme.

The limitations of one method of grouping are all the more evident when its consequences are magnified on a larger scale, over larger divisions of the form. If iambic interpretation is applied to the eight-measure sentence we have the following quantitative result:

(Each vertical line represents a bar)

This brings the greatest accent on the final or cadence measure, as Ebenezer Prout, under the Riemann influence, demands. Often, however, the content of the music seems to require exactly the reverse. The possibility of both types should be kept in mind when analyzing modern music in which there is an interplay of many forces with less emphasis upon quality or harmonic accent.

If neither iambic nor trochaic motives can be used exclusively, then both may be found in any composition; of course, as a result, motives would be of different sizes when the change from one type to the other occurred, unless overlapping is used each time.[1] Whether the theoretical designation of motives is important in practical analysis, is open to question. If we turn to the sister arts of rhythm we find prosodists who limit poetic units to three syllables (Sidney Lanier) and others who recognize non-divisible units of as many as eight.[2] The poverty of rhythmic variety in Western civilization has been blamed upon the dance; but we find teachers of the physical expression of rhythm (for example, Jacques Dalcroze in *Eurythmics*)[3] who take more complex units for granted. East Indian drummers, denied an outlet for expression along harmonic lines, perceive and perform complicated groups of **7, 11, 17** beats without referring them to a secondary subordinate grouping. The dance seems capable of great freedom in other localities and at other periods. Perhaps we should see in

ILLUSTRATION № 30
Allegretto

JACQUES DALCROZE
'50 Etudes Miniatures'
Les yeux plus grands que l'estomac

[1] Th. Wiehmayer, in *Musikalische Rhythmik und Metrik*, Magdeburg: Heinrichshofen Verlag (1917), not only does this, but he includes many more types of motives or feet derived from Greek poetry. This quotation from Beethoven will serve to show his method.

[2] Emmanuel, *Histoire de la langue musicale*, Paris: Libraire Renouard, 1911 (p. 630).
[3] Cf. Dalcroze, *Fifty Etudes miniatures* (Senart, Publisher), (*Illustrations* No. 30 and No. 31).

ILLUSTRATION № 31

JACQUES DALCROZE
'50 Etudes Miniatures'
La tortue et le lièvre

the predominance of the duple organization, in both music and dance, the decorum and the formalistic spirit of an age, which appeared in the social organization and in landscape architecture as well as in music and the figures of the court dance. In the light of all the possibilities, it would seem unwise to limit musical units to **twos** and **threes** or to one particular order of accent and *non-accent*. There has been, perhaps, a reversal of conditions; the leveling of harmonic relationships has turned the attention to rhythm as an outlet for æsthetic expression.[1]

It is true that irregularity is met most frequently at the lowest level. A real figure *three* is not found as often in a series of phrases, for the arrangement: one thesis and two antitheses, or the reverse, can be referred back to a duple basis. Any figure whatever, upon repetition, forms a duple synthesis on the next higher level, and the problem of a real 'five' in rhythmical motives without repetition is similar to the problem which Hába thought he had solved in non-repetition of content: **a b c d e**. It is this attempt to project the less usual and more complicated numbers into higher levels of the structure, which proves difficult because there is always the tendency to slip back into earlier and well-worn associations,

---

[1] This should occur at all levels in the structure and not merely in the measure. American popular music, which is supposed to be varied in rhythm, is monotonously regular at the phrase level. Not one phrase varies from the four-measure length in commercial 'Jazz.' To Gershwin's credit, some can be discovered in his opera, *Porgy and Bess*. Those who hope to use the Jazz idiom artistically are caught in this dilemma: If the four-measure phrase is retained, the larger rhetoric of the music is lacking in interest. If the four-measure phrase is made interestingly irregular, the music is no longer recognized as 'Jazz.'

a five becoming **2** and **3** or **3** and **2**, or even  rather

than five times one. An interesting illustration (No. 32) demonstrates the use of alternating measures of **4/5/4/5/4/5/4/7**. Like alternating electrical current which depends upon inequality of charge to produce motion, — or like the change of energy at the two ends of a see-saw, this device, quite apart from harmonic considerations, can set up a structure.

ILLUSTRATION N⁰32

JOSEPH SLAVENSKI
Albanischer Gesang

Lento misterioso

As a structure based upon rhythm alone can be more easily perceived the more rapid the tempo, it is to be expected that modern composers who rely upon quantitative accentual schemes would be more successful in movements of rapid tempo — scherzos, for instance. (When the emphasis was upon distinc-

77

tions in harmonic content, the pace could be more leisurely and side excursions frequent.) The result, at first, in such works as Leo Ornstein's *Poems of 1917* was a succession of regular four-measure groups of motives of extremely dissonant material in impoverished and monotonous self-generating rhythm. If we are to have eloquent irregularity in the rhetoric, we must have differentiated values in the material as well as the rhythm. Some of the new methods which set up differentiations will be considered in the next chapter. We have completed the circle of possibilities: with an intelligible rhythmic basis, we may be able to ignore to a considerable extent the demand for any other differentiation, because the rhythm produces its own synthesis and its own differentiations. If the music does not rest upon a clear rhythmic basis, qualitative accents and differentiations are necessary.

It may appear from what has been said that the 'motive' as a rhythmical unit in modern music has become a measure so elastic in length, so indecisive in its indication of an accenting nucleus, and chameleon-like in its change of content, as to defy analysis. The generating force of rhythm still operates, however, and it may be quite independent of harmonic formulæ. The use of even the most conventional cadential harmonies does not always produce a cadence. This fact is strikingly illustrated by Erik Satie in his *Pieces in the Form of a Pear;* in answer to a criticism that his music lacked form, he threw into the structure a number of Dominant-Tonic cadences. Satirically and surrealistically they have nothing to do with their surroundings, that is, with the flow of 'pure' rhythm at the moment they are used. The term surrealism is indeed appropriate here, for a typical surrealist canvas may present such unrelated forms as a piano key-board, part of last night's newspaper, a window-frame, with, let us say, a Greek column. The column may be a structural feature of architecture in some locations, but it is not one on this canvas. The same thing is true of Satie's cadences.

On the other hand, where the feature appears at its proper

ILLUSTRATION N⁰33

Allegretto

DMITRI SHOSTAKOVITCH
Prelude, N⁰20

location we have such situations as in the Shostakovitch *Prelude*
(*Illustration* No. 33), where the composer 'lands on his feet' at a
cadence like those toys which are weighted with mercury, so that

they always right themselves, no matter where they are thrown or how they are upset; we discover only after the music has finished that the point at which his sentence has landed is the point fore-ordained by the rhythmic structure, in this case, a regular sixteen motive sentence.

Dominant-Tonic successions do not produce cadences if the fundamental rhythm does not confirm them. On the other hand, the motivistic rhythm facilitates and confirms procedures which seem far from orthodox in other respects.

CHAPTER VI

NEW SYSTEMS
OF DIFFERENTIATED MATERIALS

If it is true that we should be able to discover some evidences of form in any musical work, and if form consists in some variation, however new and strange, upon the eternal theme of unity and variety, or, as the philosophers say, of the 'One and the Many,' then there must be some system in which the chaos of the many may be recognized as a tonal universe. We have been seeking to discover the orbits of circling periods in the last three chapters: First, within limits set by the weight of vertical masses of tone, or harmonies; second, by horizontal or melodic inflection which recurs in regular parallels, or in asymmetrical locations; and third, in rhythmically generated points of accent which are cumulative, but not necessarily limited to regular duple structures.

We have seen that repetition alone, either of accent, melodic inflection or harmonic mass, is sufficient to establish form. Repetition or use makes its own currency, but if we have no fixed standard of reference such as nature's system of overtones, or the system of historical tonality — which in turn is somewhat related to the overtone series, although not with scientific accuracy[1] — then each composer must establish his own method of repetition, his own individual coinage. Certain composers add to the difficulty of this obligation by changing the standard in each new composition or in each multiple form, such as the suite or sonata. Without some differentiation of materials, either natural, historical, or individual, the eloquence of irregularity is impossible.

[1] A recent attempt to relate a modified system of equal temperament to the overtone series is found in Hindemith's *Unterweisung* (Vol. I).

The right of each composition to 'live its own life' cannot be denied. We shall consider later the validity of an assumption that, as a result of this freedom, there arise new macrocosmic forms (forms-in-the-large). Inner compulsion, or propulsion to form from within, based upon the demands of the musical idea and conditioned by the notes already stated, with the 'future' related to the 'past and present' in the composition itself, can be defended against all criticism based upon external considerations. Such music is its own justification. As in the ethical problem of freedom, however, the burden of proof is upon the composer, who is 'a law unto himself.' He must establish and justify his argument; and this is a difficult task without the assistance of the harmonic relations represented in the lower end of the overtone series.

Without prejudicing the conclusion or anticipating the denouement of this chapter, it may be well to state at the outset the fundamental questions which must be kept in mind throughout the discussion. Can the newly differentiated materials proposed be used in such a way as to produce form? If the answer to this question is in the affirmative, and it is agreed that they have form-forming validity, has this result been secured in a particular composition? What are the methods used, and are there any limits in methodology which must be imposed?

To state the same questions in another form: We grant an author the right to use old words in new connections and connotations, with new insight; we permit him to 'coin words' which are necessary for his meaning; we may permit the 'stream of consciousness' to dictate the order (as it seems to do in some modern music); we may even permit the sound of words to substitute for their sense; and yet we draw the line at printers' 'pi,' and do not expect to find a poem in 'alphabet soup.' If the 'Series' and 'Tropes' discussed in this chapter are organizations which may create form, when do they lose their validity? A glib answer would be that this occurs when they lose their identity, but that needs further questioning: How should they be identified? by whom? under what conditions? We are not asking that the organization be apparent to the ordinary listener, or even to the educated listener in all its detail, after any number of hearings. We are not asking that the composer himself be aware of the details of the organization, for it is a well-known fact that analysts are able to point out to composers valid principles of organization of which the composers were not aware. We presuppose an 'ideal ear,' a supreme intelligence, but we expect that this organization, fully justified and experienced only by this ideal ear, shall in some measure appeal to the finite sense and our less perfect understanding.

The empirical manufacture of new scales has received the attention of a number of composers and theorists: Busoni, Scriabin, John Foulds, Schillinger, Vanasek, and many others. These new scales are *selections* from the twelve notes available. They are actually 'modes,' and the statements of their complete systems usually find place for the major or minor modes and the old modes as well. This chapter, however, is concerned with two attempts to utilize *all* twelve notes of the duodecuple scale without reference to what might be called modality or tonality. These are the work of two composers, Josef Matthias Hauer and Arnold Schoenberg. At the time the two systems were devised, Hauer and Schoenberg were both living in Vienna. There have been some questions raised concerning priority rights, rivalry, interrelation or influence in both directions, but these need not concern us here. That these two have established some order in the atonal chaos by setting up a system of 'Tropes' (Hauer's term) or 'Series' (*Tonreihe*, Schoenberg), has been widely heralded, but the detailed application of theory to practice has not received the analytical consideration that might well be given.

Of the two, Hauer applies his system of forty-four tropes, selecting from them, for his own compositions, the most 'fitting,' as we shall see. Schoenberg, on the other hand, redistributes his twelve tones in different allocations for different compositions or for each multiple form, and does not set up an all-inclusive system, which might have universal validity. Accordingly, we will begin with a consideration of Hauer's system.

The simplest recipe for writing atonally was stated naïvely by an American:[1] "I do not repeat any note of the twelve until I have first used all the other eleven notes." Although both Hauer and Schoenberg may seem to be adopting this facile method in that which follows, there is much more in their styles than would result from a mechanical avoidance of repetitions. To secure the differentiation of materials which we must have if the music is to be intelligibly and interestingly irregular, Hauer divides the twelve tones of the duodecuple scale into two groups of six notes each. He secures forty-four such arrangements, called Tropes. The use of this term 'Trope' is perhaps justified by one meaning given in the dictionary: "An expression changed from the original significance to another, for the sake of giving life or emphasis to an idea."

The notation which Hauer recommends for atonal music is in reality a species of tablature, in that it represents the keyboard of the piano where the lines are the black keys, and the spaces the white keys. The gaps contain two notes, b and c, or e and f. The advantage claimed for this notation is the avoidance of the use of accidentals, and of the necessity for choice between c-sharp and d-flat in a tempered notation.[2] Because of unfamiliarity, all Illustrations will be translated to the present accepted notation.

We ask if Hauer's forty-four Tropes exhaust all possibilities and do so without repetitions. For ready reference in this study we reduce the forty-four to the following series of numbers:

[1] Quoted by Henry Cowell in *Musical Resources*.
[2] The criticism that modern music is dependent upon tempered intonation — as is frankly acknowledged in the proposed tablature — and, therefore, that it is inferior to music which seems to make some concessions to the demands of pure intonation, is often made. Hindemith, however, derives pitches approximately the same as equal-temperament, from the overtone series.

NEW SYSTEMS OF DIFFERENTIATED MATERIALS

1.	1	2	3	4	5	6	7	8	9	10	11	12
2.	1	2	3	4	5	7	6	8	9	10	11	12
3.	1	2	3	4	6	7	5	8	9	10	11	12
4.	1	2	3	5	6	7	4	8	9	10	11	12
5.	1	2	4	5	6	7	3	8	9	10	11	12
6.	1	2	3	4	7	8	5	6	9	10	11	12
7.	1	2	3	6	7	8	4	5	9	10	11	12
8.	1	2	3	7	8	9	4	5	6	10	11	12
9.	1	2	3	4	6	8	5	7	9	10	11	12
10.	1	2	3	5	7	8	4	6	9	10	11	12
11.	1	2	4	5	7	8	3	6	9	10	11	12
12.	1	3	4	5	7	8	2	6	9	10	11	12
13.	1	2	4	6	7	8	3	5	9	10	11	12
14.	1	3	4	6	7	8	2	5	9	10	11	12
15.	1	2	3	5	6	8	4	7	9	10	11	12
16.	1	2	4	5	6	8	3	7	9	10	11	12
17.	1	3	4	5	6	8	2	7	9	10	11	12
18.	1	2	3	5	6	9	4	7	8	10	11	12
19.	1	2	4	5	6	9	3	7	8	10	11	12
20.	1	2	3	6	7	9	4	5	8	10	11	12
21.	1	2	5	6	7	9	3	4	8	10	11	12
22.	1	2	3	5	8	9	4	6	7	10	11	12
23.	1	2	3	6	8	9	4	5	7	10	11	12
24.	1	4	5	6	8	9	2	3	7	10	11	12
25.	1	2	4	5	8	9	3	6	7	10	11	12
26.	1	2	5	6	8	9	3	4	7	10	11	12
27.	1	2	4	5	7	9	3	6	8	10	11	12
28.	1	2	4	5	7	11	3	6	8	9	10	12
29.	1	2	4	5	9	11	3	6	7	8	10	12
30.	1	2	4	5	7	10	3	6	8	9	11	12
31.	1	2	4	5	8	10	3	6	7	9	11	12
32.	1	2	5	6	8	10	3	4	7	9	11	12
33.	1	2	5	6	8	11	3	4	7	9	10	12
34.	1	2	5	6	9	10	3	4	7	8	11	12
35.	1	2	4	6	7	9	3	5	8	10	11	12

36.	1	2	6	7	9	11	3	4	5	8	10	12
37.	1	2	4	6	7	11	3	5	8	9	10	12
38.	1	2	4	7	8	10	3	5	6	9	11	12
39.	1	2	3	5	7	9	4	6	8	10	11	12
40.	1	2	3	5	7	11	4	6	8	9	10	12
41.	1	3	5	6	8	10	2	4	7	9	11	12
42.	1	2	4	6	8	10	3	5	7	9	11	12
43.	1	3	4	6	8	10	2	5	7	9	11	12
44.	1	3	5	7	9	11	2	4	6	8	10	12

(The numbers represent the twelve notes from **C** to **B**, inclusive)

Subjecting each Trope to twelve transpositions, the forty-four produce 528 scales. However, an examination of the above Table reveals redundancy in these 528. The twelve transpositions on Tropes numbered **1, 8, 17, 19, 24, 34, 38, 41,** and **44** produce only six, three, six, six, six, two, six, six, and one distinct scale, or scales, respectively. There is no further redundancy. This reduces the 528 by 66, giving 462 distinct scales.

The mathematical theory of Permutations and Combinations reveals, as we shall show, that this is the correct number. Since the second half of each Trope is complementary to the first half, one needs only to ask: In how many ways can none, one, two, three, four, five, and six extra half-tones be inserted in a cyclic scale of six consecutive half-tone notes? The answer is:

$C(4,0)$, $C(5,1)$, $C(6,2)$, $C(7,3)$, $C(8,4)$, $C(9,5)$, and $C(10,6)$, respectively. ($C(7,3)$, for example, is a symbol that stands for the number of combinations that can be made from seven objects by taking three of them at a time.) The above series of C's give **1, 5, 15, 35, 70, 126,** and **210,** respectively. These total 462, which completes our verification.

Granted the six phases and transpositions of the Tropes to any note of the twelve: **a, a-sharp, b,** etc., it is true that any twelve-note melody can be found in one of the forty-four Tropes, and that under these conditions there can be no more than forty-four.[1] Were one to attempt to commit these forty-four to memory, there would be considerable detail to be mastered. Hauer claims, however, that he feels as much at home in them as in our scales or modes. We might liken them to East Indian *ragas* were it not for the fact that he changes the Trope frequently in the same composition. That certain Tropes are thought to be particularly suitable for certain moods is suggested in what follows. In this respect we are reminded of the fact that a certain *raga* is used for a noon-day song, but never for the morning or the evening.

Before leaving this preliminary discussion of these outlines, however, we should note that Hauer has eight Tropes, in all, which have equivalent sides or halves. These are numbers **1**, **8**, **17**, **24**, **34**, **41**, and **44**. This is obviously the case in numbers **1** and **44**. Let us see that it is also true of number **17** at the phases or re-arrangements of the second half. (The notes of the Tropes may be in any order, provided they remain in their half-trope; one might think of them as 'sheep' playing about in two fields; as long as they do not jump the fence, the two flocks keep their identity; however, they do sometimes actually 'jump the fence' in the music, and that raises some important questions, as we shall see!) In number **17**:

	7	9	10	11	12	(1)	2
is the same as:	1	3	4	5	6	(7)	8

that is, both halves present the same arrangement, and this is true of the others named.

We are now ready to see what use is made of these Tropes in the construction. Hauer distinguishes four styles:

   I. Simple twelve-note melody and homophonic accompaniment.
  II. Notes sustained, suggesting a first step toward counterpoint.
 III. Polyphonic style.
 IV. Static Tropes (divided in vertical planes).

I. In this style, a Trope is used for melody with an accompaniment selected from the same Trope. An illustration of this

---

[1] I am indebted to Dr. F. B. Wiley for the mathematical proof of that statement.

ILLUSTRATION N⁰ 34   JOSEF MATTHIAS HAUER (Op. 37)
'Fantasie'

style is quoted from Hauer (Opus 37), (*Illustration* No. 34) in
Vom Melos zur Pauke. This is not analyzed by the composer, but
we have given our analysis by Tropes as well as suggested harmonic analysis upon the old basis, in which it is seen that this

simple style, with notes doubled and with open octave and fifth in the accompaniment, is not atonal. In general, the effect is that of a succession of dominant sevenths with alterations, appoggiaturas, and passing-notes. This homophonic style is even adaptable to programmistic effects, Hauer claims, and he gives two illustra-

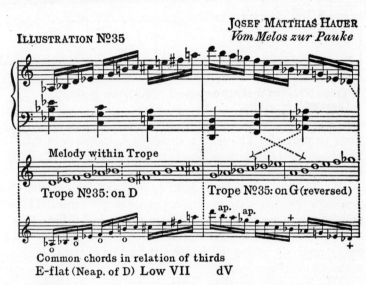

ILLUSTRATION Nº 35

JOSEF MATTHIAS HAUER
Vom Melos zur Pauke

Melody within Trope

Trope Nº 35: on D

Trope Nº 35: on G (reversed)

Common chords in relation of thirds
E-flat (Neap. of D) Low VII dV

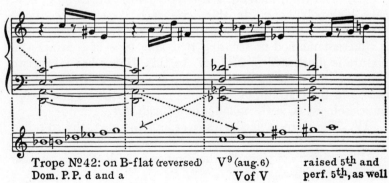

Trope Nº 42: on B-flat (reversed) V⁹ (aug. 6) raised 5th and
Dom. P. P. d and a V of V perf. 5th, as well

ILLUSTRATION No. 36

JOSEF MATTHIAS HAUER
Vom Melos zur Pauke

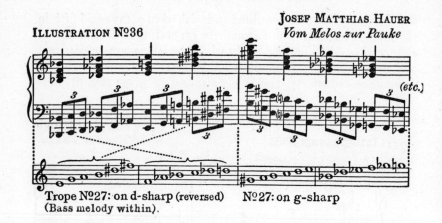

Trope No. 27: on d-sharp (reversed)   No. 27: on g-sharp
(Bass melody within).

tions to prove it: The first, a duodecuple "shower of rain" and "bird-song"[1] (*Illustration* No. 35); the second, easily related to Liszt and Wagner (*Illustration* No. 36).

II. The second method, holding over the notes of the Trope, produces the first step toward a polyphonic texture. The notes still appear in succession, each at its own point of time (*Illustration* No. 37). We have derived the Tropes and suggested a harmonic analysis, as before, which brings this example within the realm of tonal music.

III. The third method is true polyphony, or, as he calls it, *hohe*, high-polyphony. In this style each voice may continue throughout in canon or stretto (*Illustrations* No. 38 and No. 39). A different method of securing the same type of contrapuntal texture is illustrated in No. 40. In this, Hauer has taken two Tropes — numbers **31** and **40** of his system — and has divided each into three strata, or voices, as given. Each fragment continues somewhat in the manner of a *Conductus*.

IV. The third style shades over into the next, the so-called 'Static' use of the Tropes (*Illustration* No. 41). The brackets in our Illustration are given by the composer, with the information

[1] *Vom Melos zur Pauke* (p. 16).

ILLUSTRATION No 37

JOSEF MATTHIAS HAUER (Op. 37)
'Fantasie'

that inside each bracket all twelve notes are used. Some notes are held over from one bracket to the next. Although there are no sub-brackets given, the division into half-tropes in this Illustration is clearly maintained, for each quarter-note value has six of the twelve notes represented. This rhythmic distribution of the

ILLUSTRATION № 38

JOSEF MATTHIAS HAUER (Op. 37)
'Fantasie'

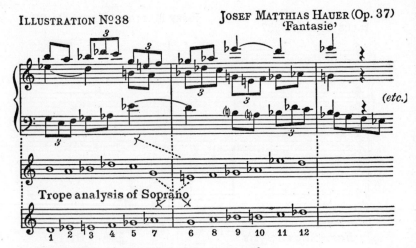

Trope analysis of Soprano

Trope №2: on D, with halves reversed

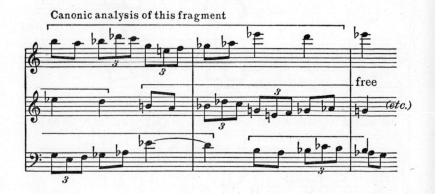

Canonic analysis of this fragment

two halves of the Trope is an important feature which we must discuss in its bearing upon form; but before doing that, we shall illustrate a more complicated development of this Fourth Style. Hauer calls it 'obstinate' counterpoint, not because of *ostinato* treatment, but because the voices are independently minded,

92

JOSEF MATTHIAS HAUER (Op. 37)
'Fantasie'

ILLUSTRATION №39

Trope analysis

Trope №23: on A (reversed)

(etc.)

Trope №27: on A

angular, or 'linear,' as in the Webern Illustration of Chapter III. This style in general is difficult to distinguish from that resulting from the use of the Schoenbergian 'Series.'

Illustration No. 42 was taken from Hauer's *Romantic Fantasie* (Opus 37) for small orchestra. He describes its conception: "Last Spring I spent Easter at Traunsee, and, as an exception, it did not rain once. The Traunstein, the lake, the meadows all conspired against the 'absolute' composer. I thought to myself: — if I could find just the right basic melodic figure, the proper Trope, then the construction of a romantic fantasy for orchestra

ILLUSTRATION № 40

JOSEF MATTHIAS HAUER
Canon

Trope № 31: on F-sharp

ILLUSTRATION № 40 *(concluded)*

Trope № 40: on B-flat

(sans program!) would be a matter of musical technique, alone. Well, I found it soon after, and in eighteen days, this opus 37 was on paper." I have quoted the composer at length to indicate his attitude in selecting the following six Tropes for this composition (*Illustration* No. 43). The basic thought is No. **24.** Each one of the six Tropes is presented in four arrangements, as given in the Illustration (No. 43). The source of the derivation is not given by Hauer, but we have added it, and stated the transpositions in each case, two perfect fifths a half-step apart. Tropes, when transposed, seem to be used as modes, but since they are composed of all twelve tones, they tend to lose their identity, and transpositions: **F**-sharp—**C**-sharp (**D**-flat), **C**—**G**, **A**—**E**, etc., indicate

95

ILLUSTRATION № 41 *(concluded)*

ILLUSTRATION N⁰ 42

JOSEF MATTHIAS HAUER (Op. 37)
'Fantasie'

Trope N⁰ 24: on F-sharp (*transposed*)

Observe the presence
(*etc.*) of an extra note (*) in
each half.

systematic transposition. (Schoenberg, in Opus 25, uses the transposition of a diminished fifth rather than a perfect fifth.)

After even this cursory examination of the use of the Trope-system in Hauer's own compositions, the question remains: In what way do the Tropes influence or produce the form? We may be able to find the 12 notes in any music, just as we may be able to find the 26 letters of the alphabet in some sentence, but this is not an evidence of form in and of itself. We have seen in Illustration No. 41 that all twelve notes are used in each half-note unit of time. The fact that they are divided between four instruments gives them less definite thematic effect than if they had been used in longer melodic atonal spans. When the Tropes appear in one voice, and when their two halves are indicated by some important rhythmical division — a measure, half-measure, etc.

ILLUSTRATION N⁰43

— then the two halves do have the effect of balance in the form, since the notes of the first half are answered by those of the second half. This is true even when the order of notes on each side of the middle, or rhythmic division, is changed. For instance, in Hauer's

ILLUSTRATION № 43 *(continued)*

Suite for Orchestra (Opus 48), the piano repeats in octaves Trope
No. **6**, eight notes to the measure, forty-eight times; however, the
order in each half is changed each time, while the notes are never
exchanged from one side to the other of the Trope. One might

ILLUSTRATION №43 *(concluded)*

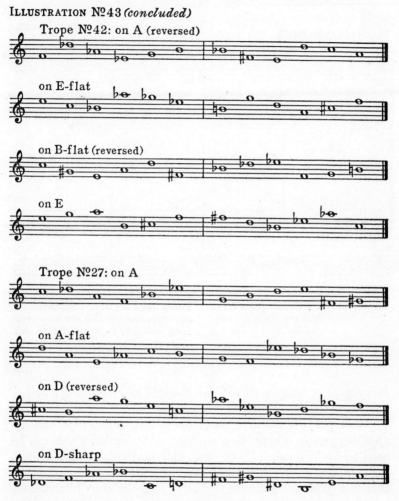

expect to find many triplets and sextuplets in music built on Tropes of twice-six notes. Although triplets are frequently used (*Illustration* No. 41) there is no limitation in the method of grouping; and when, as in this instance, three measures of $\frac{8}{8}$ use

ILLUSTRATION № 44

JOSEF MATTHIAS HAUER
Vom Melos zur Pauke

Trope №13 (as given by Hauer) Trope №43

Comments:- Two notes from first half remain in the second half.

There are nine different notes in each measure: g-b♭-c are held over from measure two, and d-flat and f-sharp are continued into measure four.

two complete Tropes, there is what might be considered a syncopation of the two-times-six arrangement.

We repeat: If the division of the twelve-note Trope into *two opposing groups* is kept, then we have a distinction which can be used to build form. (To be sure, this particular piano 'Trope-ostinato' has an effect, romantic and almost mesmeric, not unlike that of a Javanese gamelan orchestra.) If the *order* of the notes in a Trope is retained, as in a passacaglia theme, that, too, has constructive force; with rhythmic variation, some of the disadvantages of persistent ostinato are avoided; this method is not necessarily connected with the Trope system, and will be considered later. If we break down the distinction between the

ILLUSTRATION №45

JOSEF MATTHIAS HAUER (Op. 37)
'Fantasie'

Trope №18 (reversed)

The same
3 × 4
rather than
2 × 6

two halves of the Trope and, at the same time, give up repetition of an established order, we are back where we started, without any Tropes and without differentiation of materials. In this case, one 'atonal Trope' would include all possibilities.

However, this is exactly what occurs frequently in Hauer's writing. In Illustration No. 42 he admits the presence of one extra note in each half-trope phrase, but states that the phrases are still in 'equilibrium.' In our analysis of Illustration No. 44, we find two and three additional notes in almost every Trope. This, together with the fact that the Tropes are changed in each pair of measures, makes it still more difficult for the Tropes to validate the form. The change from a horizontal twice-six to three-times-four in verticals (*Illustration* No. 45) is similar to the methods of the Schoenbergian school; the Trope, as such, seems to have little influence upon the structure, since this Illustration might be as readily secured by the use of Schoenberg's Series, first horizontally and then vertically.

To conclude: If there is no evidence at all in the rhythmic structure of the characteristic division of the Trope into two halves, which might be likened to subject and predicate, or thesis and antithesis, then the Trope becomes an extremely theoretical distinction, made still more recondite by frequent transpositions and changes in the Trope numbers.

* * * * *

It appears, at first glance, that Schoenberg's 'Series' bear some resemblance to Hauer's 'Tropes.' Certainly they have received more attention, both from composers and theorists. Hauer, who dedicated *Vom Melos zur Pauke* to Schoenberg, in 1923, probably contributed more to the theory than has been acknowledged. However, the distinctions are so important that we may consider Schoenberg's 'Series' as a different method, attempting to solve the same problem. In the first place, Schoenberg makes no claim of universal application, and sets no limit to the Series as a system. Each arrangement of the twelve notes in series is valid for the particular composition of one or more movements for which it is selected. In the second place, while he may divide the Series into three groups of four notes each, these smaller 'rows' are not used in rhythmically contrasting sections with the same regularity that the Tropes often present; three-times-four division is not so important as the two-times-six of the Tropes. On the other hand, Schoenberg is more strict than Hauer in preserving the order of the notes in the Series. (As we shall see, however, this is so obscured by transpositions, inversions, augmentations, contrapuntal imitations, harmonic or vertical series, that the truth of that statement is not always evident in the practical result.)

Hauer's style is more homophonic than Schoenberg's in his later period, but the association of the latter's Series with linear counterpoint has been over-emphasized. It is true that such forms as the fugue (to be discussed in a later chapter) and the canon lend themselves to duodecuple thematic treatment, but this does not mean that the Series can be used in polyphony alone. Their most famous use in homophonic forms with vertical dramatic contrasts is in the opera *Wozzeck* by Berg.[1] The selection of the Series places self-imposed limits within which the

[1] An analysis of the forms in Alban Berg's opera, *Wozzeck*, will be found in Appendix II.

composer works. In that sense his music is more 'severe,' or strict, and has more organization than that of the extreme chromatic period which preceded. In Schoenberg's strict style there is no 'free' note; and yet there are so many variations in the way the notes may be arranged that the Series never appears twice in the same way. In other words, the organization is in the background and is not intended for conscious perception.

There seem to be two paths opening for the composer who sets out toward the elusive[1] goal of atonality: 1) Renounce all repetition with the resulting lack of form (we have seen in an earlier chapter that some who claim to have taken this road are still using repetitions of a type which they, themselves, do not choose to recognize); 2) Use such types of variation in the presentation of the same material that the repetition is not readily discovered. The avoidance of rhythmic repetitions, the avoidance of octave doublings, and the leading of Series in voices that cross at will, make it extremely difficult to follow the trail of those who use this second method. Those who object to calling this method an extension of the idea of repetition, say that any evidence of form which does not rise to the level of the hearer's consciousness does not exist in fact. This objection, if sustained, would limit the field of æsthetic theory unnecessarily, for there are many connections, influences and proportions, overtones, resultants, and compensations which do not rise to consciousness in any performance of the simplest music.

Regardless of the fact that the identification of Schoenberg's Series resembles the solution of a puzzle, it will help one to understand and evaluate the methods used if the attempt is made. Accordingly, an outline in Appendix III gives, in as complete detail as possible, the analysis of the *Prelude* of Schoenberg's *Suite für Klavier* (Opus 25),[2] and other movements of the same

---

[1] Logically, absolute atonality cannot be reached. It is as impossible as reaching for infinity.

[2] In the making of this outline, the writer has had the assistance of Erwin Stein, with whom he studied in Vienna. For its present form, however, the responsibility is assumed solely by the author of this text. As we are using the entire number, the music is not given in full, but may be secured from the **Universal Edition.**

Suite may be analyzed in the same Series, using the same general methods.

The Series selected for this *Suite* are given in Illustration No. 46. The three Series **A, B,** and **C,** use the entire twelve notes. There are eight versions of each of the three Series:

1. **Initial Series**
2. **Its transposition**
3. **The 'crab' version (beginning with the last note, reversing)**
4. **Transposition of the 'crab' version**
5. **The inversion of the series**
6. **Transposition of the inversion**
7. **The 'crab' of the inversion**
8. **Transposition of the 'crab' of the inversion**

The transpositions used are indicated by a prime (') after the letters. They are all at a distance of a diminished fifth or augmented fourth, an interval which has almost attained the position of a modern-dominant. The inversions, however, do not all take place at the same point — that of **A** starting with the first note, but that of **B** starting with the last note of **B'**. (The reason for this apparent lack of system in selecting the point at which inversion occurs may be the desire to secure more of the twelve notes in the inversions.)

To construct the Series in the first place, Schoenberg avoids, as far as possible, suggestions of tonality and turns of melody which would remind one of harmonies in the same key; however, you will note that **C**-series for this *Suite* is **B-A-C-H**; that **A** outlines a diminished seventh, and that **B** gives in its first two notes the minor third: **e**-flat, **g**-flat, followed by its encircling diminished fifth: **d**—**a**-flat. In actual composition, the notes may be distributed in any octave, since the relationships alone are binding, and not the direction of the next note or the 'voice.' Thus the minor third upward: **e'**-flat—**g'**-flat, may appear as the major sixth downward: **e'**-flat—**g**-flat. Because the Series interlock in a kind of intricate acrostic, they are not noticed, but remain in the background, influencing the texture of the entire *Suite,* and unifying the multiple form.

ILLUSTRATION №46: Series for SCHOENBERG'S Suite (Op. 25)

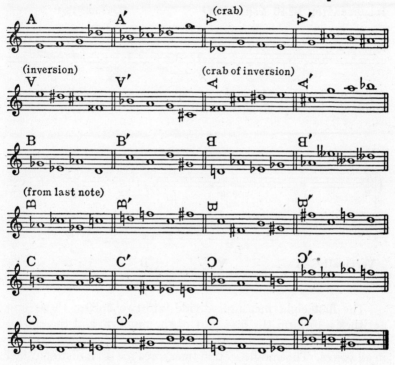

We come now to the question: What relation does the Series bear to the form itself? From the outline of the *Prelude* we see that there is considerable influence, particularly upon the large-form. At measure 17 there is a modern recapitulation, the 'Themes,' or Series, appearing in the same order as at first. Also, the interesting device of pivoting, which occurs six times in succession (measures 20–21), is a kind of condensation, or increase in density, effective in a recapitulation.

ARNOLD SCHOENBERG (Op. 25)
Suite: Prelude
Measures 10-11

ILLUSTRATION № 46 *(concluded)*

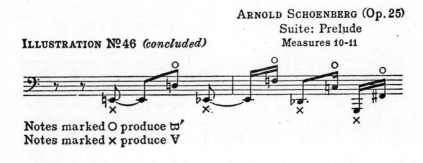

Notes marked O produce ♭'
Notes marked × produce ♭

Measure 15

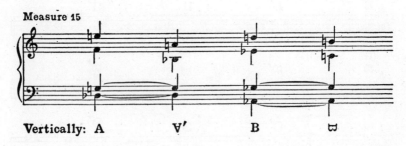

Vertically: A   ♭'   B   ♭

The first eight measures divide into two halves, thesis and antithesis, to form the first part of the number; and the end of this first section, as well as its middle cæsura, is set off by a break in all voices. The middle section (measures 10–16) is distinguished by the fact that it is not until this section that any of the Series are used vertically as well as horizontally. The close of the middle section characteristically uses figuration of almost cadenza-character, ritards and fermata.

The final section begins 'a tempo' with measure 17; although this is a little shorter, with compensating increased 'density,' the three parts are approximately equal. The number ends with the three Series in reverse order, **C, B, A**, and the final **A** Series is given as **g-f-e** in one 'chord' plus low **d**-flat.

An interesting study of the development of Series in Schoenberg's style could be made. It would, in all probability, show a

ILLUSTRATION № 47

ARNOLD SCHOENBERG (Op. 25)
Suite: Prelude
Measures 18-19

⟶ =B
┄┄⟶ =ʁ
Notes encircled: ○=B′

progressive discovery of the method; starting, perhaps, with the theme in fourths from his *Kammersymphonie,* the 'Litany' from his *Quartet* (Opus 10), and the passacaglia-like repetition of a twelve-note Series in the *Night* of *Pierrot Lunaire.*[1] It is an

---

[1] Much of this development may have been instinctive; the use of the twelve tones without repetition in the opening of Walter Piston's *Sonata for Flute and Piano* came at the dictation of the musical idea and not as conscious manipulation of the device — as the composer assured the writer.

important attempt to restore differentiation to tonal material from which all vestiges of tonality have been removed. In other words, it seeks to re-define tonality as a basis of integration. In such a complicated treatment as Illustration No. 47, the reader may be disposed to maintain that the attempt has not succeeded. When the Series bear a relationship to the form — difficult though it may be to recognize that relationship — they constitute differentiated material with new relative values produced by that very relationship.

CHAPTER VII

THE MODERN VARIATION PRINCIPLE

Vincent D'Indy, in his treatise upon composition,[1] distinguished but three manipulations which a musical idea may receive. These result in three styles, represented by three forms: the **Variation**, the **Fugue** and the **Sonata**. We must be careful, however, not to confuse the processes with the resulting forms. The methods used in Variation are also excellent methods for the development of ideas in the Sonata-form. Contrapuntal methods usually associated with the Fugue may be used in a variation.

The fundamental distinction between sets of variations and those forms based upon vertical contrasts culminating in the Sonata-form is that, in the Variation, the contrasts are between different presentations of the same idea, the form being extended by addition, while in all the forms produced by growth from monoform, through binary, ternary, and rondo, culminating in the Sonata-form, the form is produced, we may say, by multiplication and division, by germinal development and propagation with contrasting ideas. The Fugue, using methods effective for horizontal growth, produces from the given subject a gothic structure, drawing, we may say, its contrasts and conflicts from itself. Both the Sonata-form and the Fugue present solutions of the problem of unity and variety, but they approach the problem from opposite points of view. Starting with more than one idea, the Sonata-form ends with one, a reconciliation or marriage of differences; the Fugue, from the one idea, produces its manifold. All three forms — the Variation, the Fugue, and the Sonata-form — exhibit amazing vitality in their ability to adapt to changing styles. We may not wish to adopt D'Indy's generalization that they are the only forms possible, but we may well devote succes-

[1] *Cours de composition musicale,* 1902.

sive chapters to a consideration of their modern representatives.

The predilection of some of the greatest composers for the Variation — and that, when in their most advanced styles, or 'final period' — should not surprise us. Bach, Beethoven, and Brahms all show this fondness. Both Beethoven and Brahms combine more than one method of variation within the same numbered variation. What might be called a 'two-in-one' variation began as a result of the repetition of the two halves of a varied binary-form. Two or more methods were later combined within the variation of a single sentence, the first method being used for the first phrase and a different method for the antithesis. The distinction between Variation and Development as a process is broken down in such variations as the Elgar *Enigma* set, where some variations are essentially short developments based upon ideas drawn from a subject, understood or stated. Until recently, however, variations as a form have presented few problems to the analyst, particularly if he is satisfied with a superficial inspection. He had but to determine the structure of the given theme, and to state that the same form was duplicated, re-appearing in each successive variation. The important cadences recurred at the same points in all variations; in fact, in some of the freer sets, these marks of punctuation at the same points in the form seemed to be about all that was retained — the larger rhythmic form representing the stable, permanent structure of all the variations, however free they may appear to be.

One of the results of the emphasis upon variety and irregularity in the style of the present period has been a revival of interest in the Variation both as a form in itself, and as a stylistic device in other forms. Since the use of *ostinato* confers an element of unity on any material, there has been widespread use of variations on a 'ground-bass,' modern *passacaglias*, or *chaconnes*, particularly of those types which keep melodic intervals but change the rhythmic shape — the one thing that had formerly been most rigidly preserved. To be sure, there had been rhythmic-variations including some diminutions and augmentations in earlier sets, but these were usually changes in the pattern within the measure, in the lilt of the motive, often expressed in historical types of dances, rather than in the larger aspects of the rhythm. When augmented or diminished, if heard through the larger or smaller end of a musical 'telescope,' the figure was recognized as the same object. The theme, transformed as a waltz, mazurka, march, or gavot, was recognized as the same musical personality; if there was an irregularity of structure, produced perhaps by a deceptive cadence, that irregularity recurred in each variation. It is much more difficult to recognize a variation as such, when there is a radical change in the bodily structure.

We associate such bodily changes with the term 'Development' rather than Variation, since the latter has in the past been associated more frequently with superficial 'costuming.' It is true that there has been a steady improvement in the variation, involving real character-changes; but these, at least by Beethoven, were not confused with the germinal type of development which belongs in another category, according to D'Indy. The new rhythmic-variation is something different from either of these methods, being a rhythmic-variation of melodic relationships which remain fairly constant. They are related to methods discussed in the last chapter, if we recognize the Prelude of Schoenberg's *Suite* (Opus 25) as variations on his chosen Series. Aaron Copland's *Piano Variations* (1930) vary in length from 27 quarters to 49, but each may be related to the initial theme: **e**, **c**, **d**-sharp, **c**-sharp. (Incidentally, this set is in **C**-sharp-minor; with characteristic perverseness the theme is spelled with **c**-natural rather than **b**-sharp. The last chord may be analyzed by the same methods that Hindemith uses for his own music, with the result that **c**-sharp is the "best note of the best interval" of the final complex.)

If modern composers wish to use a type of repetition which will not be recognized as such, they cannot do better than to adopt the principle of rhythmic-variation. A simple illustration will suffice: We may eliminate all melody from a well-known tune,

Dixie, for instance, and yet it will be recognized by many if the rhythms alone are tapped. If we take the notes and melodic intervals, but greatly distort the rhythm, we can change it beyond the recognition of anyone. This same method of rhythmic-variation applied to a Schoenberg Series or to Hauer's Tropes may or may not be recognized, depending upon the complexity of the style as discussed in the last chapter. When it cannot be recognized by anyone, the same objections can be raised that were outlined in the last chapter. It presents the extreme to which variation as a process can be carried.

Variation, as a *form*, is important in any one of the structures which D'Indy groups under the 'Sonata'; for any repetition of a vertical section — '**A**,' for instance — need not of necessity be an exact or bald recurrence. We are familiar with various hybrids combining variation with other forms; any design which

ILLUSTRATION №48　　　　　　　HUNGARIAN FOLK-TUNE*

Tempo giusto

ILLUSTRATION №49

ARTUR SCHNABEL
Solo Violin Sonata

Langsam (*sehr frei und leidenschaftlich*)

* Quoted by Béla Bartók in *Musical Quarterly*, July, 1933.

ILLUSTRATION № 50
Allegro molto

BÉLA BARTÓK
Piano Sonata
Third Movement

ILLUSTRATION № 51 (Variation of № 50)

repeats a unit, can make use of a variation. Even in the simple ternary form, the second **A** may be a 'double' of the first. In the old Rondo, as well as in the newer Rondo-Sonata, the **A**'s were early treated as Variations, and if removed from the rest of the rondo (episodes, etc.) the result would be a Theme and Variations. It is important to make use of that fact if we are to continue to recognize these forms in present-day music. Béla Bartók quotes a folk-song from which the second theme of Sarasate's *Ungarische Zigeunerweisen* is derived,[1] which indicates that this principle is not confined to modern music. It presents a tiny ternary form in which the 'return' (the last three measures) is the type of variation of the first two measures, of which we have just been speaking. (*Illustration* No. 48.)

The same method is used for the preservation of relationships between *sections* of the *same* theme, such as the opening of Arthur Schnabel's *Solo Violin Sonata* (*Illustration* No. 49).

Bartók applies this method of variation in his *Piano Sonata* (1926) with great freedom, but the three versions of the first theme of the Third Movement (*Illustrations* No. 50, No. 51, and No. 52) can be recognized as rhythmic-variations combined with melodic decoration.

Schoenberg, in Opus 19, gives us many illustrations of this principle. The first four measures of No. 4 from this set are given in Illustration No. 53, together with their condensed recapitulation in a version, rhythmically varied in the extreme. The fact that so many recapitulations, on a scale even larger than the aphoristic Opus 19 of Schoenberg, exhibit an intensified and rhythmically shortened variation instead of a return to the first **A**, leads Bergfeld in his *Analysis of Liszt's Symphonic Poems* to speak of a 'Temporal Perspective': a shorter, more condensed version just heard, or near at hand, so to speak, seems quite as important as the longer first statement. It balances the version in the exposition because the outline and size of the first statement has become a bit indistinct in the memory and more reduced in

[1] *Musical Quarterly*, July, 1933.

ILLUSTRATION Nº 52 (Another variation of Nº 50)

(etc.)

size, the longer the time elapsing since its statement. Perhaps
this is the reason why rhythmic-variations, used as recapitulations, are usually shorter. Compare the first **A** (*Illustration* No. 54)
with the 'recapitulation' of the same (*Illustration* No. 55) in Erik
Satie's *Préamble*, from the *Cinq Grimaces* (*Le Songe d'une Nuit
d'Été*).

These modern recapitulations are but an extension of the
opportunity which Beethoven used, particularly in his last period
when treating the return of themes as a chance for further devel‑

117

ILLUSTRATION № 53

Rasch, aber leicht

ARNOLD SCHOENBERG
From Opus 19, № 4

opment. In this way the form is made more dramatic and more life-like, for history is spiral rather than circling in form; nothing recurs exactly as before. Sometimes the rhythm is maintained and the melody varied (*Illustration* No. 56); sometimes both are modified; and yet certain prominent features indicate the relationship. This is true of the second theme in Wallingford Riegger's *Blue Voyage*, the two versions of which are given in Illustration No. 57, superimposed (melody only), the one from the exposition and the other from the recapitulation.

The question of degree of variation and its limit forms the most important distinction between Schoenberg's earlier and later styles: in Opus 11 we recognize reprises because the rhythm remains (*Illustration* No. 58). In Opus 25, in spite of the fact that it is the first point in the number at which the original Series return, we do not recognize the recapitulation of the *Prelude*, because there is no return of the original rhythms. Modern psychologists state, as the result of experimentation, that the content of a return carries less weight in the verdict than the rhythm of a return. If, then, we have a return of content, but in an entirely

ILLUSTRATION № 54
A of Exposition
Modére

ERIK SATIE
Préambule
Cinq Grimaces

(etc.)

new rhythm in modern music, the composer is asking the listener
to attempt an extremely difficult task of recognition.

The critic has again retreated with his 'moving standard'.
He has agreed that the repetition, by means of which integration
is established and the circles of form completed, may be repetition of any *one* facet of the music: new vertical harmonies, melodic
inflections, or rhythmic patterns; he has further agreed that this
need not be *exact* repetition, but that it may be found in fainter
and more distant relationships or resemblance, so varied as to be
scarcely established by intellectual comparison, but, rather, only
realized by intuition. In this chapter we admit one further con-

ILLUSTRATION № 55
Entire 'Recapitulation' of № 54

ERIK SATIE
Préambule

cession: these repetitions, which are vague references, may come at irregular intervals of time, and in rhythmic patterns which bear no resemblance to those of the original statement. Further than this we cannot go. Some sort of integration, produced by some reference, at some degree of distance, we continue to demand.

There is a limit, although it may seem a vacillating and pusillanimous position, beyond which the analyst and the critic need not retreat. In the 'Theme and Variations' form we expect to find a series of varied repetitions of the same musical identity. If we do not, the composition does not deserve its name. The general shape of the original and one or two features, landmarks, or punctuations, are quite sufficient. Manifest divisions of approximately the same length, with final cadences of types already discussed, may present 'enigmas,' but we recognize the form and some slight derivation of substance. Let us examine the *Piano Variations* of Aaron Copland to see whether this set, written in 1930, is entitled to its title.

120

ILLUSTRATION №56
Allegretto

PHILLIP JARNACH
From Kleine Klavierstücke

In Recapitulation, becomes:

(etc.)

(etc.)

The theme, which is presented in a condensation on one staff in Illustration No. 59, has a structure which presents the usual features. An initial motive and the immediate repetition of that motive with one added note (the repeated **e**) form the thesis,

ILLUSTRATION Nº 57 (Condensed)

WALLINGFORD RIEGGER
'Blue Voyage'
Second Theme (melody only)

In Exposition

In Recapitulation

which is set off from the antithesis by a comma. This antithesis, which, like the thesis, is extended to five measures, has that more continuous character which we expect in an antithesis. This structure has been used so often that Alfred Lorenz refers it to early Minnesinger verse forms, and gives it a name: 'Barform,' consisting of *Stollen, Stollen, Abgesang,* or, Strophe, Strophe, Antistrophe, as we may translate it. In this form, the *Abgesang,* or Antistrophe, is twice as long as the *Stollen,* or Strophe. In characteristic German fashion, Lorenz finds this form everywhere. I once heard a lecture of his, at the University of Vienna, in which

ILLUSTRATION Nº 58

ARNOLD SCHOENBERG
From Opus 11, Nº 1

ILLUSTRATION № 59
Theme

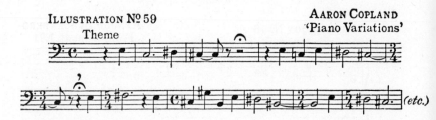

AARON COPLAND
'Piano Variations'

(etc.)

he said that the Exposition of a Beethoven Sonata-form is the *Stollen*, and that it must be repeated to form the second *Stollen*, so that the Development and the Recapitulation may be the *Abgesang!*

This well-known melodic structure is varied, with dispersions into several octaves, and with appearances in the vertical, which we usually associate with the Schoenbergian school, although Copland's connection with that school has not been emphasized. There are but seven notes in the theme proper: **e**, **c**, **d**-sharp, **c**-sharp, **d**, **f**-sharp, **g**-sharp. The notes of the motive bear a striking resemblance to the subject of the **C**-sharp-minor Fugue of Bach's *Well-Tempered Clavichord* (Book I) — **c**-sharp, **b**-sharp, **e**, **d**-sharp, **c**-sharp. To these are added successively **d**-natural, at the 'half-cadence' ending the thesis, and **f**-sharp and **g**-sharp, both in the antithesis. This highest note, **g**-sharp, comes where we are accustomed to finding the climax, about three-fourths of the way through the theme. The only other notes found in the theme are members of two accompanying harmonies, the **a**-minor and **c**-minor triads, both in their first inversions, but these are not a part of the thematic melody. If we replaced the **c**-naturals by **b**-sharps and used the signature of **c**-sharp-minor, the entire theme would be presented with no accidentals other than the usual raised leading-tone of the minor mode.

The variations are not numbered, but the cued, circled numbers coincide with the beginning of each variation, until the last; so it will be convenient to designate them by the number of the circle. The first variation is quite simple, presenting a canon in the octave of the thesis in the bass. In the second variation the features of imitative counterpoint continue, and the top staff presents for the first time a vertical order of the notes of the theme, this time, however, merely as an accompaniment (*Illustration* No. 60). These four notes of the treble-clef present the

ILLUSTRATION № 60
   (*Ibid.*) Opening of Second Variation

(*etc.*)

discovery that the opening of the theme may be telescoped into two dissonant minor-ninths (or minor-seconds, one of the minor-ninths being written as an augmented-octave — since Copland persists in writing **c**-natural for **b**-sharp).

In the third variation, the minor-second accompanies all notes of the theme, and the theme is further disguised by the use of **e**-flat for **d**-sharp and of **d**-flat for **c**-sharp.

In the fourth and fifth variations the structure or rhythmic organization as outlined above may be recognized, although the fourth variation takes place in seven measures and the fifth in nine measures, instead of the original ten measures of the theme. In other words, as long as the structure is organized in the same way (in this case, the repetition of the first motive in the thesis, followed by a more continuous antithesis, with a climax at approximately the same point — three-fourths of the way through, — falling rapidly to a cadence thereafter) the exact lengths and number of measures are relatively unimportant considerations.

With the sixth variation we meet the first transposition of the theme. Still disguised by the spelling, this presentation is in **e**-minor. Punctuating this variation, there are five groups of figures in sixteenths based upon the first four notes of the theme:

First figure:

    right hand: **g, e-flat, f-sharp, e** ⎱
    left hand: **f-sharp, e, g, e-flat** ⎰ reversed pairs in left hand

Second figure:

Same as the above, but in 'crab' version

Third figure:

    right hand: **f-sharp, e, g, e-flat** ⎱
    left hand: **g, e-flat, f-sharp, e** ⎰ voices inverted

Fourth figure:

    right hand: **e, f-sharp, e-flat, g** ⎱ Same as Third figure: voices
    left hand: **e-flat, g, e, f-sharp** ⎰ inverted and in 'crab'; or we
    may say, merely, crab version
    of First figure.

The Fifth and last figure is the same as the First figure, for 'cadential' purposes.

Variation seven is the first one in which the theme is extended through more than three octaves: G, e-flat, f^1-sharp, e^2. But it is in the same transposed key as the preceding variations.

In the eighth variation there is a 'two-in-one' effect, because the first four notes (*Illustration* No. 61) contain within the paren-

ILLUSTRATION № 61

(Ibid.) Opening of Eighth Variation

(etc.)

theses all four notes of the first motive, and at the same time the right hand contains the theme, and the left hand, the same four notes in a different order. This variation is raised to g-sharp-minor, but the ninth variation returns to the original key of c-sharp. Possibly this return was suggested by the fact that the eighth variation had been in its dominant, g-sharp.

Beginning with the tenth variation, the interest is intensified by two additional devices: the end of the tenth variation overlaps with the beginning of the eleventh, and each variation steps up the tonality one half-step. The ninth variation was in the main key, **c**-sharp, the tenth is in **d**, and the eleventh and twelfth are in **e**-flat. The final cadence of the twelfth places **g**-flat (**f**-sharp) *above* **f** to cadence on **e**-flat. The final cadence of the thirteenth variation imitates the final cadence by inversion, approaching the **e**-flat from below.

The fourteenth variation is the first in which the theme is repeated. (There are $78\frac{1}{2}$ quarter-note values, or twice the usual length.) At the end of the repetition the last measure of the variation is repeated three times for punctuation. The fifteenth variation is similar, but the punctuation is by means of a **c**-major arpeggio instead of the low **CC** pedal-point of the preceding variation. At the end of the thesis the arpeggio rises, and at the end of the antithesis it falls. The length of the fifteenth variation is not produced by repetition but by augmentation; in this case, the end note of each figure presents successively the notes of the theme, although the figure itself is also based on the theme.

In the sixteenth variation the structure of the theme is changed from a binary organization to a ternary basis. As we shall see in the next chapter, these two forms are closely related. In fact, an antithesis made of absolutely new material would give no unity to a binary form, and thus the diagram **AB** is a poor outline for this form. **A/A*** or **A/Ba** more nearly represents the usual situation. As we have already seen in Illustration No. 59, the end of our theme returns to a cadential version of the very first motive. In the sixteenth variation the last eight measures are a literal repetition of the first eight; thus the form is ternary with a rudimentary middle section. The same form is used in the seventeenth variation, but in this case the middle section is longer than the enclosing sections, which are each four measures long. The eighteenth variation is a freer adaptation of the same principle, the first and third measures of the thesis returning in the final section, but with the second and fourth measures changed.

The nineteenth variation returns to the original structure of the theme. At circle 20, which is the last cue given in the printed edition, we meet a multiple variation, an extension of the type which Beethoven used in the final variation of the first movement of the *Piano Sonata* (Opus 26) in A-flat-major. Beethoven placed several variation methods of increasing complexity in the final variation before the coda.

Discussion of this set of variations makes very uninteresting reading, as in fact does all detailed discussion of compositions apart from a musical accompaniment; however, one gains at least the impression of the degree to which relationships can be extended without complete departure from the essentials of the form.

Mahler affords one of the best introductions to the modern treatment of the Variation form, and the third movement of his *Fourth Symphony* is an excellent illustration. The theme itself is quite long: 1–8 measure, half-cadence; 9–16, another half-cadence; 16–24, half-cadence, and then, beginning with the twenty-fifth measure, the structure can be analyzed as follows: 9, 10, 11, 12, 13, 14, 15, 16, 15, 16, 15, 16, 15a, 16a, 15a, 16a, 12, 13, 14, 15, 16. At this last measure (the forty-fifth) occurs the final cadence, which is then extended: 16 equals 10, 11, 12, 13, 14, 15, 16 equals 12, 13, 14, 15, 16, 15, 16, 15, 16, 16, 16. This analysis is unimportant for our purposes, although it does illustrate again the Wagnerian method of postponing final cadences by the use of 16 and 24 as a half-cadence. The real purpose of analyzing the theme in Riemann-fashion is to contrast this with an outline of the first variation.

The very first phrase of the first variation is irregular:

1, 2, 3, 4, 5   half-cadence
6, 6, 7, 8, 9, 10   (overlap)
1, 2, 3, 4, 5, 6, 7, 8
9, 10, 11, 12, 13, 14, 15, 16   (overlap)

extended: 9, 10, 11, 12, 13, 14, 15, 16, 15, 16, 16, 16, 16, 16, 16.

Each succeeding variation becomes freer in structure. The fact that they are readily understood as variations is due to their melodic and harmonic content rather than their form, as such.

To summarize this chapter, it may be stated that a set of variations remains a cogent form provided some one aspect of the given theme is retained in each variation. As we have seen in earlier chapters, it is not a case of demanding that *all* aspects of the theme return. The burden of punctuation in modern music is borne by repetition of harmonic weight, or melodic inflection, or rhythmic generation, that is to say, by one of these with little help from the others. To these three main features of the detailed (microscopic) form we may now add the feature of the macroscopic form of the theme itself. If this last is kept, practically all features of the content may disappear in the variations; on the other hand, if we are to change the formal organization, as in the Mahler Variations, or in Numbers 16–18 of the Copland set, then we need the assistance of melodic thematic material. (In the Mahler, this is assisted by harmonic support to a greater extent than in the Copland.)

In short, the *form* has been added to the possible 'variables' in modern variations.

CHAPTER VIII

MODERN PRIMARY FORMS AND THEIR HYBRIDS

All that has been said up to this point has dealt with the detailed rhetoric of modern music *within* some type of period. Although new methods of punctuation may take the place of harmonic cadences, the musical sentence still remains as a cogent statement of a musical idea. We now consider the combination of periods or sentences, thus recognized, in the larger forms of complete compositions.

This marks a definite division in the subject. Undoubtedly, the ground that has just been covered in considerable detail presents the most radical departure in the music of the period which we have been studying, more radical than the mere increase in harmonic dissonance to which it is related, and certainly more radical than innovations in the large form considered by themselves. As evidence of this statement we have music which is extremely modern in its sentence structure but not extremely dissonant. Granted an understanding of the new types of musical sentences, it is possible to use this detailed rhetoric with its new styles of periodicity in *any* and *all* of the established forms; in fact, this is exactly what has been done in many cases. Thus we have the sonata-form in Szymanowski's three Sonatas, in the last six of Scriabin, and in Berg's Opus 1, without a 'full-cadence' harmonically from beginning to end, yet all the details of the form are clearly established; in some cases there is far greater regularity than in Beethoven's last period. Provided we are willing to admit the new type of variation suggested in the last chapter as a 'return' of the theme, we do not find the radical innovations in the large form that we have found within the sentence itself; however, there is much of interest which we hope to suggest in this chapter and in later chapters on the Sonata and Fugue.

In one sense of the word, a new form is discovered in every composition that has artistic value. Every work of art is a 'monad.' In another sense, when we examine the large forms as outlines, we find that the generic forms which musical compositions take are surprisingly limited in number; the established forms have developed through long periods of musical history, and it seems impossible to invent a new musical form overnight. There has been considerable searching of earlier history, and some revivals of baroque forms have resulted. Although certain forms seem to be particularly appropriate for certain periods of history, yet there is at least some validity, some *raison d'être*, which persists for all periods. That is, if a form presents some valid solution of the problem of unity and variety, the same methods may be used later for the organization of fresh material. At least it is a striking fact that there have been fewer innovations in the larger formal relationships than in the smaller, and most of these can be recognized as modifications in established forms.

To understand even the primary forms of modern music we need, then, the background of a thorough understanding of their appearance in past music. We must realize that there are not merely three primary forms, monoform, binary, and ternary in character, but that there are many modifications, hybrids and extensions of these forms. The word evolution would suggest too much independence as reproducing organisms, but there is a logic in the development of the forms which tempts one to use that word. We readily grant that there has been much confusion in the use of the names binary and ternary, but this confusion is the result of the great variety of types. Donald Tovey, basing his system on Parry, states that the first half of a binary form must always end with a modulation to some key other than the tonic, while the first part of a ternary form ends in the tonic, and therefore requires both a contrasting section and a return. With the disappearance of tonality, manifestly such distinctions will not hold in all cases.

If we begin with a single period we find that it may constitute the entire composition. This is true of some of the Chopin Preludes or, from the present day, Bartók's *Bagatelles* and Schoenberg's *Sechs Kleine Stücke* (Opus 19). Yet a single period, even when extended by considerable irregularity, may seem too small a canvas. In that case, three possibilities present themselves: 1) the period may be repeated (and this may demand a variation); 2) an answering period may be presented; or, finally, 3) a contrasting period may follow which demands some kind of a return for the sake of unity. If **A** represents the original period, exact repetition, or **A/A**, has the defect of too much unity; **A/B** would present too much variety. The most satisfactory solution for the simple binary form might be represented as **A′ A′**, presenting an enlargement of the thesis-antithesis already seen in the two phrases of the period itself. The second half must present some contrast, and, often, that is a matter of *direction* rather than of material idea, in that the first half modulates to the dominant and the second half returns from the dominant to the tonic, like two sides of a roof.

However, the greater the contrast at the opening of the second part, the greater the demand for a return. When this return is partial we have several types of hybrids:

A		A	is still binary in shape, but
a	a*[1]	a	ternary in content;
16	8	8	

A	A* :	A	is a binary with enlarged
16	16 :	8	second part, approaching ternary — Casella's *Minuetto* from Sonatina (1916) presents this form;

    A A* A′   is the ternary form with modified reprise (Ornstein's *Poems of 1917*, No. 1).

[1] The asterisk (*) denotes material that has been developed from that represented by the letter without the asterisk.

As the middle part approached a real 'B' in content, a more complete return of the A seemed to be demanded; but the music kept repeating the two parts as though it were a binary, even when there were three parts equal in size, and with complete balance of the first and third members. For an understanding of the differences of opinion at this point, which cause E. Prout to call the melody of *The Blue Bells of Scotland* 'binary,' and Stewart Macpherson to call the same melody 'ternary,' we need to realize that Prout looks at the form from the historical point of view. He names the 'ancestor' of the form and includes the repetition, while Macpherson takes in general the empirical approach. This is true at other points in their theories, as well.

This binary repetition of a ternary form is an interesting illustration of the evolution of forms in general; for these binary repeats were kept even when the ternary idea evolved further into the sonata-form. Certain editions of Beethoven's Piano Sonatas will show repeat marks around the development and recapitulation together, *i.e.*, around the second and third parts of the ternary idea, indicating a method of repetition that goes back not only to the immediate ancestor of the sonata-form, the ternary, but to the more remote ancestor, the binary.[1]

This binary method of repeating a ternary form gives rise to a very interesting further evolution — : A : : B A :, with the second repeat written out, becomes A B A B A, which begins to look like an early rondo form. Particularly is this true when the second B begins to go through the same process that

---

[1] These examples are in the earlier Sonatas, since the practice had been common in earlier composers. Beethoven discarded the idea, as in fact he omitted also the repeats of the exposition in more dramatic Sonatas; and yet, in the *Appassionata* (Opus 57) finale, he repeats development and recapitulation with a first and second ending. The Ignaz Moscheles edition repeats the development and recapitulation of Opus 2, No. 1 in both the first and last movements. The Paul Dukas edition repeats in the first movement but not in the last. Opus 2, No. 2, and Opus 10, No. 2, and Opus 49, No. 2 of the same edition, *repeat* — the last, however, is practically a Sonatina. In some editions the repeat in Opus 10, No. 2 is demanded by a double ending, although the content of both endings is alike. That such vestigial marks of repetition disappear by accident, as well, is illustrated by one edition in which we find them at the beginning of the development, but not at the close of the recapitulation.

changed the middle **A*** of the hybrid binary-ternary form to a **B**. **B*** becomes **C**, and the full-fledged rondo-form results: **A   B   C   A**.

We have the binary method of repeating in many different kinds of ternary forms: The middle section may be larger or smaller than the parts that enclose it. If smaller, we may consider the form ternary with a rudimentary middle section: **A | a* | A**, as in Honegger's *Sept Pièces brèves*, No. 1, where the parts are **8/5/8**. If the first and third sections are much smaller than the middle section, Alfred Lorenz gives the resulting form this interesting name: *Rahmensatz* — or 'framed-form,' because the first and last enclose the center in the proportion of border to picture. This, however, should not be confused with compositions having framing introduction and coda, since the first and last are in the main tonality and are really 'part of the picture.' Again, the middle section may present both new material and development of ideas from **A**: **A | A*** and **B | A**, but if the first and last sections balance, the form may be included in the ternary species. These are but a few of the many possibilities.

The evolution of the ternary form from the binary is a repetition on a larger scale of the oscillation set up within the measure itself. As in that case, so here there was a disturbance of balance within the binary form which produced the ternary form. After the middle section, digression **B**, the return of **A** seemed necessary, but in the ternary form **A B A**, the **B** demands again its 'place in the sun,' and after that the **A** again, and so on, *ad infinitum*. We see the same principle operating again in the sonata-form, because it is an extension of the ternary idea. If we may consider the exposition **A**, the development **B**, and the recapitulation **A**, it is again the development's turn, and this is one of the reasons why the conventional coda began to assume the character of a second development.

A reconciliation of the claims of **A** and **B** is seen in the following ternary species, where the last part is divided neatly between both themes:

A	B	A'
		A and B
16	16	8 8

The question as to which shall have the last word is avoided in Busoni's *Sonatina* (first part) where the third part reconciles the first two: **A** (1–38) **a*** (measures 39–61) **A** *with accompaniment of* **A*** (measures 62–83) Codetta (measures 84–100).

Codas to the ternary form early effected this equilibrium, and if we may think of the middle section as representing an excursion away from the tonic, we find codas exhibiting an interesting pendulum structure, thus:

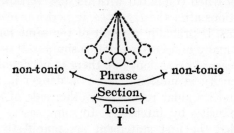

Codas early avoided sentence structure, using, at most, phrases. Their swing away from tonic had the width of a phrase at first, the tonic harmony recurring about every four measures. Then the diameter was reduced to a section (two measures), then to a measure, and finally the movement comes to a rest on an undisturbed tonic harmony.

The character of the second **A** in the ternary form was discussed in the last chapter in connection with the new type of variation. This, too, is only relatively 'new,' as composers realized that a literal repetition was anti-dramatic, or at least at variance with life itself. In the earlier days, manuscript paper and ink, to say nothing of the composer's time, were too valuable to be spent in re-copying. To be sure, the *Da Capo* returns, associated with the Neapolitan school of opera composers, have supplied another name for this form; but the composers of absolute music usually changed their reprises, presenting either a climaxed version, or one of falling action. Sometimes, this was used with temporal perspective, which accepts a shortened version because it is nearer to us in the 'falling action.' On the other hand, a shortened version may be justified by an intensification of the style. Tension or intensity seems to compensate for the lack in extension. A simple illustration is found in those ternary forms in which the first **A** presents material in succession which in the recapitulation becomes a duet between two 'voices' and, therefore, requires but half the space in time. The last **A** in the Second Movement of Mahler's First Symphony shows aural foreshortening when compared with its first version. The omission of repetitions after the *Da Capo*, in performances of Minuet and Trio forms, is probably a result of the same logic.

However, many numbers are not so simple. It is easy for the analyst to measure extension, but there is no definite measurement for intensity in music. There is a danger in reading into every brief and irregular return, the other side of an equation, balancing extensity by intensity. In some cases, irregularities which extended the first statement are manifestly omitted in the return. The form is determined as a rule not on the basis of actual extension but upon the weight of the musical material when the irregularities have been reduced to regularity; that is, an irregular eight-measure period of fourteen measures has the same 'weight' as a regular eight-measure period. Even when this allowance is made, the returns in modern music frequently do not agree in extent with the first statements. In analysis, there is the same desire to avoid the designation, 'asymmetrical,' that there is to avoid the label, 'atonal.' Critics in the other arts have coined the term 'dynamic-symmetry'; perhaps they know how to use it in their arts. We would like to use it in music, but it rests upon such subjective units that we cannot demonstrate the truth of the equation. We may point to the fact that the melody rises to a higher climax, or that the style is more compact, the dynamics more extreme, but we then have to be satisfied with the statement that as far as we are concerned, in this particular case, intensity compensates for a lack in extension and establishes a true equilibrium in forms which, at first glance, appear to lack proportion on paper.

A 'recapitulation by substitution' is perhaps stretching the meaning of the term, and yet that seems to be the best designation for the second '**A**' in the Second Movement of Stravinsky's *Piano Sonata* (1924): **A** (measures 1–12), **B** (13–39) and **A**^{2} (40–52) in which only the first two measures are like the first **A**. In this case, however, Stravinsky is in his 'neo-classical phase,' and is using the tonic key for **A**^{2}. The repetition of tonality is sufficient compensation.

The 'reversed return' is used frequently in modern music. We shall see in the next chapter that the second subject often returns before the first, in sonata-recapitulations. Lorenz has the apt name: *Bogen*, or 'Arch,' for this form; the units in an arch are reversed in order on each side of the key-stone, 'reading from left to right.' However, the arch is still in blocks or segments. A true 'crab' return is less usual; for instance, the famous 'crab' *action* of Hindemith's *Hin und Zurück* is not accompanied by any literal crab-version of the music. Programmatic reasons probably suggested this type of return to Poulenc in his *En Voiture* of the set *Promenades*, the scenery appearing in reverse order on the return trip. In Piston's *Concerto for Orchestra*, second movement, the theme reappears in retrograde motion in the reprise.

In all of the primary forms discussed thus far, we have expected to find some evidence of unity in the form. Joachim Bergfeld would add to these varieties a 'Series' form **A B C D . . .**, non-repeating in character, and he feels that he needs this form in the *Analysis of Liszt's Symphonic Poems*. If useful there, a form of this character would seem doubly useful for modern music. However, it is possible to present other analyses for the Liszt Poems, and to discover basic unity which seems absent in the Series outline in modern music, if we are willing to accept the more distant relationships discussed in the last chapter. It is even more difficult to listen to five or seven radically different content-groups, without establishing relationships, than it is to listen to five or seven beats without imposing an accented pattern.

Our excuse for this long digression from the consideration of definite illustrations of modern compositions lies in the fact that most of the hybrids which have existed in the past can be observed in the music of to-day. For instance, composers are again writing in all the embryo stages of the sonata-form as' well as in the classical version. A recapitulation beginning in the subdominant, so that the exposition's **I–V** may be recapitulated as **IV–I**, has as much merit as it ever had. (Perhaps it foreshadows the pivoting about an 'axis' which we shall find to be an important modern type of recapitulation.) Each step, historically, was more or less complete in itself, and is justified on æsthetic grounds; it gave, and still gives, æsthetic satisfaction. It is true that the regular ternary form has been used more widely, but there is much to be said in favor of ternary forms with varying proportions; a variety of solutions can be secured. The question might arise in the mind of a theorist: Is there any 'optimum' relationship between the two parts of a ternary form, between the length of the **A** and the **B**? Could experiments be devised similar to those described by Bosanquet,[1] which Fechner conducted upon the basis of the 'Golden Section' principle of Zeising? Using a perfect square and then changing the figure to rectangles of varying sizes — some of which were almost square, while others were much longer in one direction — he found an agreement in preference for the rectangle based on the 'golden section,' in which the lesser side is to the greater as the greater is to the sum of the two sides. Fechner gave as his measurements $21:34$, but when we figure the equation we find that this is not an exact result. The equation is still one-1870th away from a true equation. Bosanquet does not intimate the fact, but the formula $\left(\dfrac{x}{y} \text{ equals } \dfrac{y}{x \text{ and } y} \right)$ works out to an irrational number.

[1] *History of Æsthetics.*

If a perfect 'Golden Section Rectangle' is impossible, this fact may represent the unattainable perfection of form in art itself. There does seem to be some validity in a middle section which stands to the first and last sections of a musical ternary form in rough approximation to the relation 5 to 3, which approaches that of the best rectangle. Just as the eye in some way measures objects in view, approving or rejecting proportions, so the ear estimates extensions and proportions in a musical form without mechanical counting. However, any comparison of the behavior of the two senses in such an operation would be a difficult problem in psychology, and probably could not be set up on a scientific basis.

In order that we may compare the first and last divisions of a modern ternary form with the middle division, we must discover two important points: 1) the close of the first part as determined not only by the presence of some of the substitutes for the cadence discussed in Chapters III–VI, but also by the entrance of what is recognized as contrasting material, and (2) the point at which some type of reprise begins. This last is usually marked by a return to the initial idea, but this is difficult for the ear to recognize when the return, as in the third number of the first of Ernst Krenek's *Two Suites*, is an exact 'crab' of the first. This is a perfect 'Lorenz-arch' in every detail, but when we approach the return 'end-on' it cannot be understood aurally as readily as 'on paper.' Musical forms are addressed to the ear.

CHAPTER IX

THE MODERN SONATA

The title 'Sonata' has been given to many different types of composition from the sixteenth century to the present. In books on musical Form and Analysis, the term has also been used as a *genus:* the String Quartet being defined as "a sonata for two violins, viola, and violoncello"; the Concerto and the Symphony, as "sonatas for orchestra, with or without soloists." Two main types have been recognized, the 'Old Sonata' and the 'Modern Sonata,' the distinguishing mark of the latter being the appearance, usually in the first movement, of a highly organized form, based on the contrast and development of two main subjects. This form, unfortunately, was called 'Sonata-form';[1] the choice was unfortunate because it is then necessary to explain that, as a rule, Sonata-form is not the form of a sonata. Because 'Sonata-form' is the form of one movement considered as a unit (with certain modern exceptions to be discussed in this chapter), the form of a sonata is equivalent to Sonata-form only in the situation where the sonata is in one movement and that movement is in Sonata-form. We must hasten to add that there are many modern sonatas which contain *no* movement in Sonata-form, as well as some which contain as many Sonata-forms as there are movements! There seems, then, to be little that can be stated concerning a sonata without the necessity of qualification, beyond the fact that it is an instrumental work of 'high seriousness.' This may seem to lack definition, and yet the absence of this qualification is often a sufficient ground for denying the title. The sonata remains one of the three fundamental generic types and,

[1] That the theorist has been a notorious laggard in keeping pace with the changing forms of music is indicated by William S. Newman's paper on the 'Recognition of Sonata-form' (*Proceedings* of the Music Teachers National Association for 1941) in which he states that, as late as 1840, Carl Czerny believed he was outlining Sonata-form for the first time.

as such, it has exhibited a remarkable adaptation to changing styles. It has survived the disappearance of the older harmonic cadence, and it may be expected to continue in use as long as vertical distinctions and a hierarchy of values in musical materials remain.

The modern sonata presents two important problems which are more fundamental than any questions of nomenclature: First, the problem of reconciling the increased importance of the Sonata-form, if that is used as the form of one movement, with the multiple form of several movements; and, second, the problem of a recapitulation in the Sonata-form for a generation which may consider a reprise based upon a strict unity of tonality unnecessary (in other words, the problem of the *form of the Sonata* and the problem of the *Sonata-form*, if we may continue to use this confusing distinction). Modern music has made certain contributions toward a solution of both of these problems, which will now be considered in that order.

Albert S. Chandler[1] has given a descriptive program of a sonata for the general reader, which uses the familiar analogy of a hero and heroine. This reference is cited not for the purpose of demonstrating the absurdity of a program — which Dr. Chandler himself admits — but rather to point out the non-recognition, in the program, of the first movement as a completed drama: in the recapitulation, the hero "returns triumphant, expecting to win the hand of his beloved." The slow movement continues: "Coldly received by his beloved," and so on. There is the consequent extension of a romantic story containing two characters through the remaining movements. Absurd as this may be, a dilemma somewhat similar, although stated in purely musical terms, is faced when a multiple-movement sonata opens with a completed Sonata-form in the first movement.

The problem was not a critical one in the early sonata or suite, in which all the forms were binary or binary-ternary hybrids. It can scarcely be said that it arose before the nine-

[1] In *Beauty and Human Nature* (p. 205), Appleton-Century, 1935.

teenth century had greatly increased the dramatic character of the first movement, and at the same time added more contrast in the themes and tonalities of the other movements. The fact that all movements of the older suite were kept in the same key, with two main choices for the modulation at the end of the first part of each movement, in itself produced sufficient unity. The power of tonality is still used in many modern sonatas, operating, however, over the entire span of movements. For instance, the Dutch composer William Pijper opens and closes his *Trio for Piano, Violin, and Violoncello* (1921) with the **C**-major triad, but he carefully avoids any conclusion of the drama at the end of the first of the three movements by a chord spelled: **D A f b e**^{1}. Through the simple expedient of avoiding a cadence in **C** until the end of the entire work, the circle of the cycle is kept open. Most composers have depended upon more substantial solutions. Some of these are so famous, and belong so definitely to the nineteenth century, that we will list them without detailed comment:

1) Unity has been secured by cross-reference and quotation; this has often been combined with the abolition of distinct pauses between movements, either by the use of transitions or merely by directions for performers to continue without pause.

2) *L'idée fixe* of Berlioz and the *ego* themes of Liszt present musical personalities which continue in various guises, determined possibly by the program, throughout the movements of the form.

3) Both of the above were developed into a more extended system, which may be called 'cyclical treatment,' culminating in an accumulation of material in the final movement. César Franck is noted for this solution, and he has had many followers.

We come now to methods which are more closely associated with the twentieth century. There is a growing recognition of the fact that the logic of the form is complete in the first movement. If this is so, why add more? As a result, the twentieth century has seen an increase in the number of sonatas written in one movement and, as a natural consequence, an increase in the size of that one movement. The Scriabin sonatas, from the *Fifth* on, are good illustrations of this solution. Long introductions containing more than one important idea, and codas, frequently in the nature of a second development, round out the form. The final section of the second subject is often so different from the other sections as to deserve to be called a third subject; the bridge between the first and second subjects is extended, and contains new themes which increase the cast of characters. The one-movement Sonata-form was early adopted for overtures and symphonic-poems, but its use — with no suggestion of a program for such a work as Alban Berg's *Piano Sonata* — is characteristic of a solution which avoids the difficulty by omitting the remaining movements of a multiple form.

The most interesting development of the twentieth century has been the attempt to solve the problem by the interlocking or intermingling of the constituent parts of forms or movements. The moods and the tempos of first movement, slow movement, and brilliant finale often have been connected in concertos, but this newer solution is not so much a matter of through-composition as a matter of the inter-relation of sections of forms. Theophil Stengel[1] indicates but one concerto which might be cited as a forerunner of the interlocking of movements: Frederick Delius *Piano Concerto in C-minor* (1897), in which the slow movement, appears between the exposition and the recapitulation of a Sonata-form. The two middle movements have frequently been combined; for Beethoven, the Trio of the Scherzo often served to present the mood of a slow movement, and the opposite arrangement is found in the middle movement of the César Franck *Symphony in D-minor*. Carrying the Delius plan further, the *Sonata for Clarinet and Piano* of Paul Juon appears to be in one movement, but introduces an embryonic slow movement, Scherzo, and even 'Finale' — if this last term can be used here to designate a type and not a location — *between* the exposition and the recapitulation of a Sonata-form. In terms of the story used

[1] In *Die Entwicklung des Klavierkonzerts von Liszt bis zur Gegenwart*, 1940.

by Dr. Chandler, this, at least, has the advantage of postponing the 'wedding' until after all the other action — which he describes — occurs.

A more 'orderly' solution is that of Schoenberg's *Kammer-symphonie* in which the 'slow movement' appears between the exposition and the development, and the 'scherzo' between the development and the recapitulation; all of this occurs, of course, without pause for movements, and with considerable cross-reference of thematic material. More radical is the presentation of the exposition and its recapitulation as two separate movements in Hindemith's first *Sonata for Piano* (1936). The exposition, set apart by Roman numeral I, is recapitulated in reverse order of themes, as Movement IV, two complete movements intervening. The use of a reversed recapitulation is logical. The elements of an 'arch' are repeated in reverse order as we follow its line.[1] However, the division of the historical form into movements so widely separated seems less satisfactory than a more closely integrated structure of diverse elements in one movement.

In Hindemith's *Sonata for Viola and Piano* (Opus 11, No. 4), the second movement is a Theme and Variations in which we hear the theme and four variations as a movement; then, without pause, we have the exposition of the Sonata-form of the Finale with its two contrasting subjects; instead of development, we have more variations of the second movement and then the recapitulation of the Finale, ending with another complete variation in the Coda. Such interlocking of the forms of various movements represents a new and interesting attempt to solve the sonata problem as a whole.

The second problem to be considered concerns the recapitula- of the Sonata-form — a form which until recently was confined within the borders of a single movement. Some of the characteristics of its earlier history reappear in the present period, and there is every justification for their reappearance. We may

---

[1] So frequently has this type of recapitulation occurred that Alfred Lorenz has given it the name '*volkommene Bogen*' in his study of the forms in Wagner's 'Ring,' *Das Geheimnis der Form* (Vol. I), 1924.

recognize the various ancestors of the Sonata-form as outlined by Stewart Macpherson,[1] and yet we so often fail to realize that the evolution of this form, and in fact of all forms, is still continuing in their descendants of the present generation. On the other hand, we may make the mistake, which is equally disastrous, of failing to recognize the reappearance of the earlier stages of the forms in modern music. The term evolution, as used here, does not imply that later developments are more satisfactory, æsthetically, than earlier forms; the term merely emphasizes the fact, underlying the title of this volume, that forms change. Each stage in the Sonata-form, or in any other form, has presented its own solution for the problems of unity and variety. Therefore, they remain valid, and we may expect them to reappear in modern content. For instance, there was a time in which the development section was present as a short digression at the opening of the second part of the form; earlier still, it was practically non-existent. In the twentieth century, much of the modern Sonata-form is in the style of development; and the openness of structure, which first appeared as a characteristic of the middle part of the form, has now been extended to exposition and recapitulation as well. Thus the development as a separate section tends to disappear. It was in the development sections of earlier sonatas that listeners discovered that they did not have to have full cadences for cogency. In that sense, they were the most 'modern' sections of the forms.

The feature of the modern sonata which we shall now discuss, namely, the use of more than one tonal center for the recapitulation, is but the revival of one of the earlier stages of the form with certain new features. The first subject at one time appeared in the subdominant in the recapitulation. This had advantages: it made possible a literal transposition of the exposition a fourth higher for the recapitulation, and the same bridge served as well for both. Schubert's early *Symphony in B-flat-major* (No. 5), first movement (1815), is a late example of the same procedure.

[1] *Form in Music* (Chapter XXV), London: Joseph Williams (Revised edition, 1930).

In the modern period, this use of different tonal centers for the two subjects of the recapitulation has returned, not for purposes of facile transposition, but for added variety and interest in the final section of the form. Several types may be cited. In the *Sonata for Viola and Piano* by Hindemith, mentioned above, both the first and second subjects of the recapitulation occur one whole tone higher than their first appearance in the exposition. In Scriabin's *Fifth Sonata* both subjects are transposed up a fourth. These transpositions to a higher location may have for their purpose the heightening of effect in the recapitulation. Note, however, that Scriabin's use of a fourth for this purpose produces the same result as we found in Schubert's *Symphony*.

Of greater importance is the growing use by Hindemith of an axis-relationship for the second subject, in which the theme is presented in the recapitulation at the same distance *above* the first subject as it was presented *below* that subject in the exposition. Even when it is not possible to speak of tonalities in the old sense in connection with first and second subjects, this procedure can still be recognized by the interval of transposition in relation to what might be called the polarity of the first subject. This plan was foreshadowed in Beethoven's *Waldstein Sonata* (Opus 53), where the second subject of the exposition, of a Sonata-form in C-major, starts in E-major, and in the recapitulation appears for a few measures in A-major before returning to C. Note, however, that one interval is a major third and the other a minor third. In the modern procedure, as used by Hindemith, the interval is usually an exact distance; Beethoven's choice for the recapitulation is below the tonic, while Hindemith's, as a rule, is above the main tonal center. In the first movement of the recent *Sonata for Viola and Piano* (1940) the first subject is on F, in which tonality the movement also ends, according to Hindemith's method of determining tonality — as explained in his *Unterweisung im Tonsatz*. The second subject at measure 32 begins on E in the exposition, and the same subject begins on F-sharp in the recapitulation. These locations are a half-step, respectively, below and above the tonal center of the movement.

In Hindemith's *Sonata for Flute and Piano* (1936), first movement, the tonality of the first subject is unmistakably **B**-flat major. The key of the opening of the second subject of the exposition, marked "ein wenig ruhiger," is **G**-sharp. In the recapitulation the key of the beginning of the second subject is **C** (same tempo mark). These are one whole step below and above 'tonic.' It is quite a matter of indifference to Hindemith — as it is to most modern composers — that the first interval is a diminished third and the latter a major second. In the *Sonata for Violin and Piano* (1935) the first subject is in **E**-major and the second subject of the exposition (at cue-letter **A**) is in **E**-flat. We expect the second subject of the recapitulation to be in **F**, and this is the case, although the situation is complicated by the fact that the second returns before the first (two measures before cue-letter **D**). The relationship, as in the case of the first illustration, is below and above, but here, a half-step. The second movement also exhibits polarity. The real movement begins "Sehr lebhaft" at measure 36, in **E**. The second subject at measure 70 is in **E**-flat; the reversed recapitulation introduces the second subject on **F** at measure 151, and the final **A** at measure 193, beginning a minor third lower than **E**, reaches the main tonal center at measure 210. The first movement of the *Sonata for Oboe and Piano* (1938) begins and ends on **G** as a tonal center. The second subject, at measure 37, is on **F**-sharp; and in the reversed recapitulation, at measure 134, the second subject reappears, changed in rhythm, but based on **A**-flat. What might be called a closing theme of the exposition starts on **F**-sharp and ends on **E**; this is answered in the recapitulation according to the usual method for groups of keys in a second subject, by **A** and **G**. The main second subject is a half-step lower and a half-step higher than the principal axis of the movement.

Perhaps sufficient examples have been cited to indicate that this new procedure should be admitted as a feature of Hindemith's Sonata-forms, although there are many in which it does not occur. In summary, may we repeat that the location beneath the axis comes in the exposition and the location above and at the same actual distance, regardless of the way the interval may be notated, occurs in the recapitulation. When we begin to look for theoretical justification of this new procedure, several interesting possibilities may be suggested. Hindemith has not discussed the large forms in the two volumes of his *Unterweisung*, published thus far, and the following are tentative suggestions if justification seems needed. An interest in counterpoint and a revival of the modes may have suggested an extension of the relationships in the *clausula vera* (step-wise motion to a cadence from opposite sides of a final) to larger divisions of the form. If the older relationships of perfect fifths and fourths are predominantly harmonic in effect, the relationship of major and minor seconds agrees with Hindemith's emphasis upon the *Sekundengang*, or melodic nuclei a step apart. If recognition of thematic personalities, or '*Gestalten*,' is an important consideration, the results of an experiment conducted by Andor Juhasz[1] may have a bearing on the situation. Apparently, this writer has established the principle that transpositions of short melodic series are recognized most frequently as the same forms, or '*Gestalten*,' previously heard, if transposed a fourth or a fifth; next most frequently, if transposed a second or a seventh, and least frequently, if transposed a third or sixth. These were 'real' transpositions, not 'tonal' ones, and they were mixed with new series until some 120 series were used. They were 'nonsense-series,' unrelated so far as possible to known melodies, according to Juhasz; as the series were not printed in the report, it is impossible to pass judgment on the validity of the conclusion. The report is cited because a recapitulation of the second subject a whole or half step above the location in which we had come to expect its appearance might be considered a repetition by substitution, the memory adjusting subconsciously to the new location. It may be of interest in this

[1] Reported in *Zeitschrift für Psychologie, 95* (pp. 142–180), 1924, under the title: *Zur Analyse des musikalischen Wiedererkennens*.

connection to anticipate the next chapter on the Fugue, where we shall find Hindemith using the relationship of a second for the reappearance of the subject in fugal expositions. In both exposition and counter-exposition of the Finale of the *Third Piano Sonata*, the same three centers of tonic, dominant, and supertonic are used for the entrance of subject, answer, and subject. Some underlying cause may be leading to an increasing importance in the relationship of a second for both sonata- and fugal-forms.

The reversed recapitulation, in which the second subject comes before the first, was not unknown, of course, in the nineteenth century. In the twentieth it becomes almost the rule rather than the exception. Bridges, as such, are disappearing; in a style characterized by open structures, with the relationship of any and all tonal centers to any given point recognized, the necessity for formal bridges or transitions needs no longer be maintained. With the revival of the *concertato* style and Baroque forms, the mere juxtaposition of a series of ideas does not seem to demand recapitulation. Thus, some modern sonatas make no use of the Sonata-form; however, those which do include it offer interesting solutions for the two problems discussed in this chapter. They have as their purpose the integration of the sonata as a whole by means of the interlocking or fusion of the forms of individual movements, and the creation of a freer and more modern recapitulation, or *dénouement*, for the most important single form involved.

That these are not final and definitive solutions may be taken for granted in this art, which does not draw its forms from the objective world.

CHAPTER X

THE FUGUE IN MODERN MUSIC

We now come to a consideration of the last of the three fundamental generic types, the Variation, the Sonata, and the Fugue. In terms of historical origin and designation, the order in which we have discussed these may be criticized, but from the standpoint of neo-classical, neo-polyphonic, 'Back-to-Bach-and-Beyond' movements, there is no topic that is more opportune to-day. We may substitute for the names of these three forms the generic processes back of them, and state that, given a musical idea, there are three fundamental procedures which may be used, if a form of some type is to result: 1) we may repeat the idea with a difference (variation); 2) we may develop some part or all of the idea in a process of germination, induced by its inherent potentiality acting within its environment (the environment in the Sonata-form is in part, at least, furnished by conflict and contrast with other musical ideas), and (3) we may imitate it and extend its ramifications in a horizontal structure of more than one stratum; that is, we may present the idea in contrapuntal 'flight' or fugue.

Stated in this way, it is obvious that these three types are perennials, and we should not be surprised to find all of them exhibiting great vitality in the present period. The continuous rhetoric of the Fugue, in particular, may be recognized as modern in its essential method. Cadences have always been more or less obscured in the contrapuntal forms, and the various contrapuntal devices have effective validity even when the thematic material approaches atonal or extremely 'linear'[1] counterpoint. We must acknowledge that these three processes have not

---

[1] This term used by E. Kurth in *Grundlagen des Linearen Kontrapunkts* (1917), is, in reality, tautological, but has proven useful in its emphasis upon melodic considerations as compared with harmonic coincidences.

been kept distinct in the present period, and perhaps there is no reason why they should be. We have seen in the chapter on the Variation that the outlines of the themes have disappeared in some modern variations and, as a result, "A Set of Developments Based upon a Theme" might be a more appropriate title. Contrapuntal treatment is possible, of course, in any form or in any part of a form, and it is especially effective in developments. That Beethoven's last period sought a coalition of the Sonata and the Fugue is a well-known generalization.[1] Although the Fugue itself is usually outlined on a ternary basis, some of Bach's fugues are more nearly binary than ternary, and there is no reason why a fugue in rondo-form should not be written. It has been pointed out that the *Grand Fugue* (in B-flat, Opus 133), by Beethoven, is in Sonata-form.[2]

It is not our purpose to review the details of the Fugal-form, but certain features will need to be discussed in their bearing upon modern adaptations. The subject of the fugue presents at the outset the musical idea from which the entire work develops. This, also,—in the past, at least,—has presented at the same time the tonality of the fugue, either the tonic key itself, or the tonic and dominant keys, or the reverse; and finally, on rare occasions, the dominant alone (in which case the tonic follows, iambically, we might say, in the answer 'at the fourth'). All of the advice, suggestions, or 'rules' for tonal answers, which cause so much confusion in the minds of students, have as their purpose the preservation of a strong feeling of tonality during the exposition. If more than one key occurs, the relation of any and all other tonal centers must be recognized as subordinate to that one. Chromatic subjects in no wise disturbed the situation. In Bach's

---

[1] This presents either a general enrichment of texture (Opus 111), or the use of canonic and fugato sections and complete fugues (Opus 106).

[2] Hermann Scherchen in *Die Musik*, XX, 6 Marz (p. 405), 1928. The double exposition in B-flat and G-flat corresponds to the two thematic groups of a Sonata-form exposition. The development is in A-flat-major, beginning 'Allegro molto e con brio.' The last section begins with the second 'Allegro molto e con brio,' and Coda with the third. For more specific details the original article should be consulted.

Chromatic Fantasie and Fugue, the fugue is considerably less chromatic than the fantasie, and the chromaticism occurs between what might be considered the 'upright supports' of important chordal tones. In counterpoint, dissonance gradually increased as it was recognized that 'point against point' and not 'note against note' was satisfactory. However, one must wait for modern music to hear again the dissonance of simultaneity in the degree to which this was used in the thirteenth century. The clashing sevenths of Strauss's *Heldenleben* are a logical extension of the counterpoint of the *Meistersinger*, and point forward to Milhaud.

In the fugue, although the harmonies resulting from more chromatic subjects became more elaborate, the exposition remained tightly organized architecturally. The recurrence of alternate entries in tonic and dominant became increasingly chromatic with any tendency to tangential divergence prevented, if necessary, by the use of tonal answers. In the romantic period such fugal expositions were frequently used in the development sections for a program which involved the 'working-out' of themes. The *Purgatory* section of the *Divine Comedy* gives Liszt the excuse, if one is needed, for the theme, as well as the soul, to "work out its salvation." In *Prometheus* and in *Faust*, chromatic expositions, or fugato sections, are introduced for similar reasons.

When the subjects become not only more chromatic but at the same time less related to harmonic poles within the structure, that is, when they approach an atonal idiom, the exposition may be kept on 'even keel' by entries in the fifth and fourth, and yet the result may lack any strong feeling of tonal center. An example of such a chromatic subject is found in the Sorabji Fugue (from *Prelude, Interlude, and Fugue* — 1924), which contains eight of the twelve tones before one is repeated: B-flat, B, C, F-sharp, C-sharp, D-sharp, E-sharp, G. But a change much more radical, so far as the 'architecture' of the Fugue is concerned, is the introduction in this case of subjects and answers in the exposition at intervals other than those of dominant and tonic. This is of course not a new procedure and many examples can be found in the early history of the development of the form from the Ricercare, and in the famous example of Beethoven in the Finale of the *Pianoforte Sonata* (Opus 101). Here the subject is not chromatic, and the unity of tonality is skillfully maintained in spite of entries at the third, etc.

The student composing a fugue is told to use the tonal answer for a subject which modulates from tonic to dominant, because "if a real answer is used, this would take you to the super-tonic tonality," and the structure would not remain in the 'perpendicular,' but would look more like the architecture sometimes seen in pictures or in stage-sets. Architects are prevented from such freedom or license of fancy in plans for actual construction by the law of gravity.

Willi Apel asks whether the third, fourth and fifth entries in the exposition may be in the fifth of the preceding, *i.e.* **C, G, D, A** for subject, answer, subject, answer, and then answers his own question: "That would mean a violation of the sense of tonality and a failure to recognize the law of the Fugue — therefore, we must return in the third voice to **C** (the first tonality)."[1] And yet this series of entries in successive keys is exactly what Richard Strauss has used in *Also Sprach Zarathustra*, where the entries start successively with **C, G, D, A** and **E** (this last, the 'head' only of the subject). This is as tangential as the circle of fifths, and possibly the program has again influenced the choices: the section is labelled "Von der Wissenschaft," and this key scheme may be intended to indicate Nietzsche's pessimistic fear that Science gets progressively farther and farther from the truth or center (**C**-major) the more involved it becomes. This departure, however, which was quite unusual in the day when *Zarathustra* was written, is not an uncommon practice in present-day fugues. Sometimes the first two entries start in the traditional tonic and dominant, and then the third voice, wishing to avoid exact repetition, answers at another interval. In Hindemith's *Third Piano Sonata* (Finale) there is an illustration of the use of but one tangential entry. We have seen in this composer's treatment

[1] Willi Apel: *Die Fuge* (p. 17), 1932.

153

of the key scheme of his sonata recapitulations the importance which he gives to the super-tonic tonal center. In this fugal finale, the architecture of the exposition is reinforced by a Counter-exposition which uses the same three centers of Tonic, Dominant, and Supertonic for subject, answer and subject. This procedure, particularly when strengthened by repetition, seems much less radical than expositions involving more than three centers. It also avoids the danger of the use in the exposition of so many different locations for entries that there is little left for use in the middle section. This is similar, of course, to other dilemmas which we have already discussed: If all harmonies can be inter-preted as dominant, or as dissonant or non-cadencing structures of the 'thirteenth,' what have we left for other denominations, and what differentiations of value remain in the harmonic hierarchy? If all is development, will the climax be as effective, or the *dénouement* as satisfying as in a form using greater differen-tiation?

The objection may be raised that these two types of modern fugal expositions are in effect the same, being (1) an 'atonal' subject with what might be called tonal or conventional exposi-tion in the fifth and fourth, and (2) a less 'atonal' subject; that is, a *chromatic* subject (using the term *chromaticism* to mean recognizable, though fairly radical, relationships to tonal centers within the subject itself) on which an exposition is written at intervals other than the conventional fifth and fourth. This is not, however, the case. The two methods are distinct and differ-ent in effect. Since the configuration or *Gestalt* of the fugue subject is more clearly recognized as such in the second type, it may be considered the less radical procedure. In either case, the necessity for the modifications associated with the 'tonal' answer is no longer apparent, and that type of distinction tends to disappear in modern fugues.

The reason that so much emphasis has been placed upon new types of exposition in this discussion of the modern fugue is that the middle and final sections have always been remarkably free in modulation; no two of Bach's fugues are alike, and there is much greater freedom in the form than the outlines of a 'School-fugue' would indicate. There will always remain the demand for a subject which can be recognized as a structural unit throughout the rest of the fugue. To change the figure: if the middle section of a fugue presents fluidic movement — an 'ocean' on which we may travel to arrive at entries of the subject — then these entries, or 'islands,' must be recognized as configurations. It is possible that continued experience with duo-decuple music may enable the listener to check subconsciously the number and order of the notes as they appear in any thread of the argument, such as the answer of a fugue. But until that time arrives, subjects integrated about tonal centers and expressed with rhythmic individuality prove most effective. To mention the Strauss subject in *Zarathustra*, again: all twelve notes were used, but each section of three notes outlined a common major or minor triad or inversion. It is possible to use twelve tones in succession with many varying degrees of tonal integration.

In many cyclic works, at the present time, the point of greatest emphasis has changed from the first movement to the finale. Szymanowski has made effective use of fugues in the last movements of his second and third Piano Sonatas. His *String Quartet* (Opus 56) also ends with a fugue in which the first answer is at the fifth; and the third entrance, which used to be called the subject — perhaps we need to revise these names if the distinction disappears — again is in the minor 'seventh,' and the final entrance in the perfect 'fourth' — speaking in terms of intervallic distance from the original location. Note, however, that these are really two pairs of entries, a whole step apart, of the same subject in the *fifth*. Again, as in the Hindemith Sonata, we find a procedure which gives more unity to the exposition than to the middle section. In the final section of this fugue the subject returns in its original tonal location, but three octaves higher, and *fortississimo*.

With the increasing dissonance that is characteristic of linear counterpoint, it would seem that *stretti* no longer present the same problems as before. Actually the problems remain in the necessity of avoiding rhythmic and harmonic coincidences. Too conspicuous harmonic or rhythmic agreement seems like a patch of old cloth on a new garment. The individuality of the voices must be maintained; this is facilitated in fugues written for instrumental groups by a modern type of instrumentation and orchestration in which non-blending colors help to keep the contrapuntal strands distinct.

The revival of interest in the technical methods of polyphony may be the result of far more fundamental causes than any 'Back-to-Bach' movement, or a mere reaction against romanticism. Erwin Stein said, in 1925:[1] "A coördinating principle has not yet been found. It is scarcely possible that any such may develop from the theory of harmony; rather — (we may expect it) from melodic theory." Walter Harburger[2] goes so far as to imply that atonal music must be polyphonic: "A single melodic line may form an atonal arabesque, and many melodic lines may create atonal counterpoint; but homophonic music depends upon real cadences of some sort and, therefore, *cannot* be atonal."

With a reinterpretation of what is meant by cadence in homophonic music, the limitation implied in Harburger's statement seems too sweeping; and yet it is true that polyphonic devices retain their effectiveness even when the material becomes quite dissonant. With such aids as augmentation, diminution, the crab-version, and inversions, music may be written with freedom of rhythm and an apparent disregard for resulting clashes of vertical coincidence.

The Passacaglia and the Chaconne also present to the modern composer a comparatively easy solution for the problem of form. Given the repetition of a ground-bass figure, the unity of the form follows ready-made, as it were, because the composer may play above the fundamental unity in free, or even wayward, improvisation without the possibility of the charge that the law of unity — at least the 'letter of the law' — has been violated.

[1] *Von Neuer Musik*, F. J. Marçan Verlag.
[2] 'Musical Geometry,' *Zeitschrift für Musikwissenschaft* (January, 1929).

This method, however, was used to excess in the decade 1920 to 1930, when it became almost an ultra-modern mannerism, and recently there has not been so much recourse to its too-easy solution of the problem. With the increase in dissonance in popular music, the so-called 'Boogie-woogie bass' answers the same purpose.[1]

We need not underestimate the great variety of mood and emotional content in fugues by Bach, Brahms, or Busoni; and yet we must admit that there is some justification for the generally accepted opinion that contrapuntal forms make a greater and more nearly continuous demand upon mental perception than homophonic forms. If it is true that atonal music is most effectively written in polyphonic style, we should not be surprised that this music is accused of being constructivistic, mathematical or mechanical. Modern music, however, is no more limited to the horizontal point of view than was previous music. The Fugue in Berg's *Wozzeck* accompanies an emotional, psychologically complex scene of great intensity. The horizontal and vertical emphases have continually brought enrichment to their opposites in style. The fundamental vertical presented in the overtone series brought with it the possibility of organum and polyphony. Even polytonality may be said to be inherent in a single-line melody at the level of the second overtone. In contrapuntal suspensions, and the telescoping of delayed neighboring chords with their resolutions, many modern harmonies have been discovered. A real canon at any other interval than the octave points toward bi-tonality and the increasing tonal independence of modern counterpoint. In music, to-day as always, it is not a question of *either* polyphonic *or* homophonic styles, but of *both* polyphonic *and* homophonic styles, with the proportional emphasis shifting at different periods and with different composers.

It is doubtless true that contrapuntal methods and devices are able to lend a specious unity to the most unpromising, or

[1] Those who look for the influence of 'Jazz' upon more artistic music will discover that the contributions, or 'appropriations' — to use a polite word — have been in the other direction, for the most part.

seemingly most disorganized, material. This may offer a ready solution for the detailed carpentry of the style, but the larger architecture is still dependent upon the recognition of total centers, related in some way which indicates their relative importance. Both homophonic and polyphonic forms have been composed of material which is increasingly dissonant. To state that music which approaches atonality must make use of contrapuntal devices exclusively, is to set up an unnecessary limitation. It is true that chromaticism was historically a horizontal development, and that dissonances arrived as melodic decoration long before they were named as harmonic effects. Although the fugue and other contrapuntal forms do not represent all the possibilities, they are extremely important in the present period and will remain important in the future development of music.

CHAPTER XI

IN CONCLUSION

The evidence which has been presented indicates that modern music is not without form. A changing material vocabulary has brought about changes in the methods of punctuating, but the necessity for cogent periodicity remains. It is impossible for the composer to escape the obligations imposed by the very nature of the art. As Dante has said, any production of tones for the enjoyment of their relations is Music.[1]

If we are baffled when we are seeking unity and relation at one level in the structure, we should look for it at another. If it is not to be discovered in the measure of the motive, we may find it at a 'higher' level in the larger unit of the phrase, or in the 'lower' level of the figure.[2] When the basis of organization is not obvious at first hearing in a self-generating rhythm, we may look for it in melodic inflection or in the repetitions of harmonic weight. In reality, all three bases are still present, but they may not seem to coöperate so obviously in contemporaneous music as they have at other periods.

Following the general discussion of the first three chapters, we have avoided, as far as possible, the difficult problem of values in modern music in the hope that we may indicate methods for understanding the grammar and rhetoric of the style, leaving final judgments — as they must always be left — to individual taste. If we agree with Goethe[3] that it is when working within limits that mastery is revealed, we will recognize the important part which the limitations of form play in the creation of a master-

---

[1] Dante: *Convito* II, Chapter XIV.

[2] This has been indicated in the analyses of music by Cyril Scott and Alois Hába, respectively.

[3] "In der Beschränkung zeigt sich erst der Meister
   Und der Gesetz nur kann uns Freiheit geben"
   — 'Epigrammatische' *Natur und Kunst.*

piece. In literature, the Sonnet-forms have presented such limitations, and they have challenged poets in many languages. In somewhat the same way, cadenced structures and fugal expositions in music still have their challenge for the modern composer. It has been frequently pointed out that it is possible to base comparisons of nineteenth century composers solely upon the originality and beauty of their cadences. The same focal points may be used as a basis of judgment in contemporaneous music, provided we recognize changing methods of punctuation. The verdicts of the future will not be based primarily upon analysis, but we may be sure that a cogent articulation, a *Gestalt-*organism, intuitively effective, will be a prerequisite for the award of merit. Rhythm, as a synonym for such an organizing principle, is the very life of a composition, and can no more be explained in all its completeness than we can explain Life itself.

"Natura non fecit saltus" and art does not know 'halves.' To be sure, nature sometimes strays from the norm and produces those animals which find their way to the collection of 'freaks' in the circus. It must be admitted that some music written since 1900 may belong in this group; but we must be careful to distinguish irregular, but well-articulated forms, from those that present an apparent symmetry which is half good musical tissue and half padding. A thorough acquaintance is sometimes necessary before we are able to express an opinion. Memorization, or the test of performance, may help to confirm or deny inherent values in the music. Even here we must try to distinguish between pleasure in accomplishment — the satisfaction of efficiency in performance, or in listening habits — and the enjoyment of the music itself. One of the objections which seek to invalidate our judgments of modern music is expressed in the statement that "it is possible to get used to anything," even to the noises of a modern factory. Yet there is no substitute for thorough acquaintance, renewed after intervals, as a basis of judgment. The judgments of history depend upon this slow and fallible process. These, too, are subject to change.

History appears to move in cycles. One is tempted to point to parallels in such diagrams as the following:

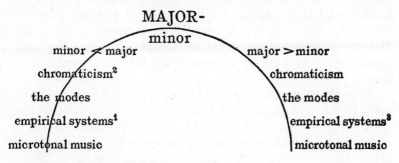

MAJOR-
minor

minor < major   major > minor

chromaticism[2]   chromaticism

the modes   the modes

empirical systems[1]   empirical systems[3]

microtonal music   microtonal music

[1] Ragas; melodic multiplicity; zanze scales; etc.
[2] Gesualdo; Marenzio.
[3] Busoni; Scriabin; etc.

'Tyranny of Bar-line'

Counterpoint-of-bar-lines   Measures of varying sizes

Measures of varying sizes   Counterpoint-of-bar-lines

No bar-lines   No bar-lines

Some would say that the logical implication of such parallels is in the direction of a return to the primitive; but this would place too much emphasis upon superficial aspects of style. Periodicity depends upon principles of organization which are of a more fundamental nature than the regular recurrence of bar-lines. There have been many tonal systems and there may be many more.

The individual and distinctively personal expression does run the risk of a limited appeal. Music in Western Europe has been a 'universal language' based upon certain harmonic relationships widely accepted; one who attempts to create a new language runs the risk of being misunderstood. Propaganda and publicity are called upon for their help, but they often confuse the issue, pitting one specific style against another. In a period of neo-classicism there is a demand for neo-romanticism; but more fundamental than any *ism* for romantic and classical music — for music with a program or without a program, for music diatonic or pandiatonic, tonal or atonal — remains the basic consideration of form as a prerequisite for communication in music.

It would be absurd to attempt to solve the problem of æsthetic value in the final chapter of a book on morphology. To describe what happens when we hear great music, such technical terms as *catharsis* or *Einfühlung* are scarcely more useful than the words of our American poet, Sidney Lanier, flutist in an early Baltimore symphony:[1]

To Beethoven

I know not how, I care not why
Thy music sets my heart at ease,
And melts my passion's mortal cry
In satisfying symphonies.

*   *   *   *   *

Yea, it forgives me all my sins,
Fits life to love like rhyme to rhyme,
And tunes the task each day begins
By the last trumpet note of time.

The logical realist may wish to dismiss these verses as romantic mysticism, and yet the poet has here suggested the character of the æsthetic experience which we expect from great music, and which we have the right to expect from at least some of the music that is being written in our own day and generation.

This book is based upon the author's experiences of æsthetic satisfaction in modern music and the convictions which resulted therefrom. To ask him to list those particular works which have

[1] Taken from a longer poem, published in *Poems of Sidney Lanier*, by **Charles Scribner's Sons.**

given him the greatest satisfaction would be to demand an auto-
biographical confession of personal judgments which are still
changing, a confession which would be of little value to another.
Values there are, however, to be recognized in the music of our
own day by intelligent listening, and it is in the hope of aiding
in their recognition, that this book has been written.

APPENDIX

I. ANALYSIS OF SCRIABIN'S **Fifth Sonata for Piano**

II. ANALYSIS OF ALBAN BERG'S OPERA: **'Wozzeck'**

III. ANALYSIS OF SCHOENBERG'S 'PRELUDE' FROM THE **'Suite für Klavier'** (Opus 25)

I. Analysis of Scriabin's
Fifth Sonata for Piano

Illustrating the application of older methods of structural analysis to a composition in which the conventional harmonic cadence has disappeared.

Introduction (*Impetuoso*):

> 1, 2, 3, 4, 3, 4, 3, 3, 4, 4, 4, 4
> (*Languido*)
> 1, 2, 3, 4, 5, 6, 7, 8, 5, 6, 7, 8
> 1, 2, 3, 4, 5, 6, 7, 8, 8
> 1, 2, 3, 4, 1, 2, 3, 4, 5, 6, 7, 8, 8

Exposition (*Presto*):

A:

> 1, 2, 3, 3, 4, 4: 5, 6, 7, 7, 8, 8
> 9, 10, 11, 12, 13, 14, 15, 16, 16

Bridge Passage:

> 1, 2, 3, 3, 4, 4, 5, 6, 7, 7, 8, 8
> 9, 10, 11, 12, 13, 14, 15, 16
> 1, 2, 3, 4, 5, 6, 7, 8

> New theme in Bridge (*Imperioso*)
> 1, 2, 3, 4, 5, 6, 7, 8
> 9, 10, 11, 12, 11, 12, 13a, 14a, 13b, 14b, 15, 15, 16, 16, 16, 16

B₁:

> 1, 2, 3, 4, 5, 6, 7, 8
> 9, 10, 11, 12, 11, 12, 13, 14, 15, 16, 13, 14, 15, 16, 16

B₂:

> 1, 2, 3, 4, 1, 2, 3, 3, 4, 4, 3, 3, 4, 4

Introduction (*Impetuoso*):

1, 2, 3, 4, 4, 4, 4, 4, 4

(*Languido*)

1, 2, 3, 4, 5, 6, 7, 8, 5, 6, 7, 8, 5, 6, 7, 8, 8, 8, 8

Development:

1, 2, 3, 4, 4, 4, 1, 2, 3, 4, 1, 2, 3, 4, 1, 2, 3, 4, 1, 2, 3, 4

1, 2, 3, 4, 5, 6, 7, 8, 5, 6, 7, 8

1, 2, 3, 4, 5, 6, 7, 8

1, 2, 3, 4, 5, 6, 7, 8

1, 2, 3, 4, 5, 6, 7, 8, 1, 2, 3, 4

1, 2, 3, 4, 1, 2, 1, 2, 3, 4, 5, 6, 7, 8, 8, 8

(*Meno vivo*)

1, 2, 3, 4, 5, 6, 7, 8

1, 2, 3, 4, 5, 6, 7, 8

1, 2, 3, 4

1, 2, 3, 4

1, 2, 3, 4, 3, 4, 5, 6, 7, 8

1, 2, 3, 4, 5, 6, 7, 8

1, 2, 3, 4, 5, 6, 7, 8

1, 2, 3, 4

1, 2, 3, 4, 5, 6, 7, 8, 5, 6, 7, 8

Recapitulation (*Prestissimo*):

A: (Merging with Bridge)

1, 2, 3, 3, 4, 4: 5, 6, 7, 7, 8, 8

9, 10, 11, 12, 13, 14, 15, 16

1, 2, 3, 4, 5, 6, 7, 8

Imperioso theme in Bridge

1, 2, 3, 4, 5, 6, 7, 8

9, 10, 11, 12, 11, 12, 13a, 14a, 13b, 14b, 15, 15, 16, 16, 16, 16

B$_1$:

1, 2, 3, 4, 5, 6, 7, 8

9, 10, 11, 12, 11, 12, 13, 14, 15, 16, 13, 14, 15, 16

B₂: Merging with Coda (***Allegro***). The first two measures
overlap with the last two measures of B₁.

1, 2, 1, 2, 3, 4, 3, 4, 5, 6, 5, 6, 7, 8, 7, 8
1, 2, 3, 4, 5, 6, 7, 8
9, 10, 11, 12, 13, 14, 15, 16
1, 2, 3, 4, 5, 6, 7, 8
1, 2, 3, 4, 5, 6, 7, 8, 7, 8
1, 2, 3, 4, 4, 4

II. ANALYSIS OF THE FORMS
IN ALBAN BERG'S OPERA: 'WOZZECK'

A copy of the following outline of Alban Berg's 'Wozzeck'
was given the author by Erwin Stein, with whom he was studying at the time. As it presents the Forms with great precision
and, in all probability, reflects the composer's intention, it is
included here.

FORMS, ETC.

ACT I: **Five Character-Pieces**
The 'CAPTAIN' — a **Suite**

PAGE of Piano Score		MEASURE
9 SCENE I	Præludium	1
	Sarabande	30
	Cadenza (Viola)	51
	Gigue	65
	Cadenza (Contra-bassoon)	109
	Gavotte	115
	Double I	127
	Double II	133
	Aria	136
	Reprise of Præludium in 'crab'	153
27 Entr'acte	Finale (development of Suite ideas)	173

MEASURE

30 Scene II.....................'Andres' — Rhapsodie,
over a succession of
three chords........... 201
to which is added a
three-verse Hunting-
Song of 'Andres'...... 213
249
259
40 **Entr'acte**.....................Coda of Rhapsodie 303
and beginning of
Military music behind
the scenes............ 326
41 Scene III....................'Marie' — Military
March............... 332
Cradle-Song Introduc-
tion................. 363
Cradle-Song.......... 372
Scene between 'Marie'
and 'Wozzeck'....... 427
54 **Entr'acte**.....................Transition........... 473
55 Scene IV.....................The 'Doctor' — Passacaglia (or Chaconne)
21 variations......... 488
73 **Entr'acte**.....................Transition........... 556
74 Scene V.....................The 'Drum-major' —
Andante affetuoso...... 667

ACT II: A Symphony in Five Movements
82 Scene I.....................Introduction.......... 1
83 **First Movement:** Sonata-form: Exposition 7
Repeated Exposition.. 60
Development......... 96
Recapitulation........ 128
94 **Entr'acte**.....................Continuation of Recapitulation and Coda. 141
97 Scene II **Second Movement:** Fantasie and Fugue on
three themes:
The first two themes... 171
The third theme....... 273
The Fugue........... 286

MEASURE

124 **Entr'acte**.................... Coda of Fugue and Introduction of following 363
124 SCENE III **Third Movement:** Largo for Chamber-
orchestra............. 367

(The Chamber-orchestra uses the same instrumentation as SCHOENBERG'S
Kammersymphonie, Opus 9.)

135 **Entr'acte — Fourth Movement:** Scherzo I (*Laendler*) ... 412
137 SCENE IV.................... Trio I............... 456
Scherzo II (*Walzer*).... 481
Trio II............. 561
Scherzo I (Quasi Re-
prise, with Dialogue and
basso ostinato)........ 592
Trio III (Quasi Reprise
of Trio I)............ 605
Scherzo II (Quasi Re-
prise of *Walzer*........ 671
and development of the
same)............... 685
164 **Entr'acte** .... Introduction to final
Movement........... 737
170 SCENE V **Fifth Movement:** Rondo with Introduction 742
Rondo martiale...... 761

ACT III: Six Inventions

181 SCENE I.................. 1. **On a Theme:** 1
Seven Variations..... 10
Fugue.............. 52
188 **Entr'acte**.................... Conclusion of the Fugue
189 SCENE II................. 2. **On a Tone:**
Pedal-point, *crescendo*
on B-natural........ 71
197 **Entr'acte**.................... Transition to next Scene 109
198 SCENE III................. 3. **On a Rhythm:**
Fast Polka........... 122
Drinking-Song........ 145
'MARGARET'S' Song ... 169
Ensemble............ 186
208 **Entr'acte**.................... Continuation of the
above, quasi develop-
ment............... 212

MEASURE

210 SCENE IV................4. **On a Six-note Chord:**
(A-sharp, C-sharp, E-
sharp, G-sharp, E-flat,
F-flat)............... 220
Placed on other steps.. 267
Coda............... 284

224 **Entr'acte**................5. **On a Tonality** (D-minor,
quasi epilogue)....... 320

229 SCENE V................6. **On equal movement** in
eighth-notes, quasi Toc-
cata................ 372

III. ANALYSIS OF SCHOENBERG'S 'PRELUDE' FROM THE 'Suite für Klavier' (Opus 25)

Series

Measure 1: Soprano: **e, f, g, d**-flat .... **A**
Bass starts: **b**-flat, **c**-flat... **A′**

Measure 2: Soprano: **g**-flat, **e**-flat, **a**-
flat, **d**............... **B**
Alto starts: **b, c, a, b**-flat... **C**
Tenor starts: **c, a, d, g**-sharp **B′**
Bass ends: **d**-flat, **g**....... **A′**
Bass starts: **f, f**-sharp, **e**-flat,
e.................... **C′**

Measure 3: Alto ends: **b, c, a, b**-flat.... **C**
Tenor ends: **c, a, d, g**-sharp **B′**
Bass ends: **f, f**-sharp, **e**-
flat, **e**............... **C′**
Soprano starts: **a**-flat, **c**-flat,
g-flat, **c**............. ꓭ

Measure 4: Soprano ends above **Series**
Alto: **e**-flat, **d, f, e**........ ꓳ
Bass starts: **b**-flat, **a, g, d**-
flat.................. Ɐ′ (Last note in Soprano)

Measure 5: Soprano: **g, d**-flat, **c**-flat, **b**-
flat................. Ɐ′
Tenor: **a**-flat, **d, a, c**....... ꓭ′
Bass: **e, e**-flat, **f**-sharp, **f**... ꓛ′
Bass: **d**-flat, **g, f, e** .... Ɐ (Last note in next meas-
ure)

172

Measure 6: Soprano starts: **f**-sharp, **c,**
             f, d.................. ଧ′ (First note also Tenor)
        Alto: **a**-sharp, **b, g**-sharp, **a** ꓛ′
        Tenor: **d, a**-flat, **e**-flat, **f**-
           sharp................. Я (Last note in Soprano)
        Bass: **b**-flat, **a, c, b**....... Ɔ (Last note in Alto)
        Bass: **g, d**-flat, **e**-flat, **e**.... ◁ (First note in octave)

Measure 7: Soprano ends: **f**-sharp, **c, f, d** ଧ′
        Alto: **b**-flat, **c**-flat, **d**-flat, **g** A′
        Alto: **c, a, d, a**-flat........ B′
        Bass: **e, f, g, d**-flat........ A
        Soprano: **e, e**-flat, **d**-flat, **g** ∀ (With Alto in next
                             measure)

Measure 8: Alto ends: **c, a, d, a**-flat.... B′
        Soprano: **f, g**-flat, **e**-flat, **f**-flat C′
        Tenor: **d, f, c, g**-flat....... ꟽ′ (Last two notes in next
                             measure)

        Bass: **g**-flat, **e**-flat, **a**-flat, **d** B
        Bass: **b, c, a, b**-flat........ C

Middle Section
Etwas ruhiger

Measure 9: Soprano ends: **f, g**-flat, **e**-
           flat, **f**-flat............ C′
        Alto: **d, f, c, g**-flat .... ꟽ′
        Bass: **a, a**-flat, **c**-flat, **b**-flat ꓛ′
        Soprano: **d**-flat, **g, a, b**-flat ◁′
        Tenor: **c, e, g**-flat, **f, b, d,**
           a-flat, **e**-flat............ (*See* Illustration No. 46)
        (Combines two **Series,** alternately)

Measure 10: Soprano ends: **d**-flat, **g, a, b**-
           flat.................. ◁′
        Soprano starts: **d**-flat, **g, f, e** ⩛
        Bass: **e, d, e**-flat, **f, d**-flat, **c,**
           g, f-sharp............. (*See* Illustration No. 46)
        (Combines two **Series,** alternately)
        Tenor: **a, a**-flat, **c**-flat, **b**-flat ꓛ′ (Set off by accents)

Measure 11: Tenor ends above **Series**
Soprano ends: **d**-flat, **g, f, e** Ɐ
Alto: **d**, **a**-flat, **e**-flat, **g**-flat ꓭ

At this point, Vertical Combinations within **Series** enter for the first time in this number. They will be indicated within parentheses.

Soprano and Alto: (**b**-flat,
  a) **c, b**................ Ɔ
Tenor and Bass: **e**, (**d**-flat,
  f) **g**................ A
Soprano and Alto: (**g**-flat,
  e-flat) **a**-flat, **d**........ B (Last two notes in meas-
                                    ure 12)

Measure 12: Soprano ends above **Series**
Bass: **b**, (**a, c**) **b**-flat....... C
Soprano and Alto: (**b**-flat,
  a) **g, d**-flat............ Ɐ′
Tenor and Alto: (**b, g**-sharp
  and (**f**-sharp, **c**)........ ꓭ (First time as two pairs)
Bass: **e**-flat, **d, f, e**........ Ɔ

Measure 13: Soprano and Alto: (**a, g**-
  sharp) and (**b**-flat, **c**-flat) Ɔ′ (Only **Series** of 4 half-
Tenor: **d**-flat, **f, c, f**-sharp   tones)

Note: If the first tone were **d**-natural, then this would be **Series B**. Since there is no major third in any **Series**, Erwin Stein stated that this is undoubtedly a misprint, and that the note should be **d**-natural.

Soprano: **d, f, c, f**-sharp.... ꓭ′ (Last two note sinnext
                          measure)
Bass: **e**, **e**-flat, **d**-flat, **g**.... Ɐ (First note from meas-
                          ure 12)
Tenor: **g, d**-flat, **e**-flat, **e**... ◁
Bass: **b**-flat, **c**-flat, **a**-flat, **a** Ɔ′

Measure 14: Soprano: **d, f, c, f**-sharp ... ꓭ′
Bass: **b**-flat, **c**-flat, **d**-flat, **g** A′

Measure 15: (*See* Illustration No. 46)

Measure 16: Soprano: **b**-flat, **c**-flat, **d**-
  flat, **g**................ A′
Alto and Tenor: (**e**-flat, **d**)
  and (**f, e**)............ Ɔ
Soprano: (**b**-flat, **c**-flat, and
  Bass: **a, c**)............ Ɔ (B–A–C–H)

Recapitulation

Measure 17: Tenor: **e, f, g,** d-flat ...... **A**

Bass: **g**-flat, **e**-flat, **a**-flat, **d** **B**

Bass: **b, c, a,** b-flat........ **C**

Soprano: **c, a, d,** g-sharp **B'**

Alto: **f, f**-sharp, **e**-flat, **e** ... **C'**

Measures 18, 19: (*See* Illustration No. 47, in the text)

Measure 20: Soprano: **e, f, g,** d-flat, **f, e** . **A** (Doubled, using **g,** d-flat, twice)

Alto: **g**-flat, **e**-flat, **a**-flat, **d,** e-flat, **g**-flat.......... **B** (Doubled — same device)

Bass: **b, c, a,** b-flat, **a, c, b** .. **C** (Doubled, on b-flat as a pivot)

Measure 21: Soprano: e-flat, **d, f, e, f, d,** e-flat................ ꓛ (Doubled, on **e** as a pivot, but transposed a diminished fourth)

Alto: **a**-flat, **c**-flat, **g**-flat, **c,** **g**-flat, **c**-flat, **a**-flat...... ꓭ (Same device)

Bass: **b**-flat, **a, g,** d-flat, **g,** **a,** b-flat.............. Ɐ' (Same device)

Measure 22: Alto: **d, a**-flat; Tenor: **e**-flat; Alto: **f**-sharp.......... ꓭ

Soprano: **f, c, a,** f-sharp, **d,** e-flat, a-flat, **e**........ **C'** and **B'** (underscored)

Tenor: **e,** e-flat; Bass: d-flat, **g**.............. Ɐ

Bass: **b**-flat, **c**-flat, **d**-flat, **g** **A'**

Alto: **a**-flat, **a, c**-flat, b-flat ꓳ '

Measures 23 and 24 bear little relation to the **Series** in any obvious vertical or horizontal order. However, the last four notes form **A**, while **B** and **C**, reversed, may be found in the last half-measure:

Alto: **b**-flat, **a**; Tenor: **c**; Alto: **b**.............. ꓳ

Tenor: **d**; Soprano: g-sharp, e-flat, f-sharp .... ꓭ

INDEX

A

Albanischer Gesang (Slavenski), 77
Also sprach Zarathustra (Strauss, R.), 153, 155
APEL, WILLI, 153–154

B

BACH, J. S., 2, 33, 73, 112, 124, 150–151, 154, 156–157
Bagatelles (Bartók), 132
BARTÓK, BÉLA, 4, 36–37, 66–67, 71–72, 114–117, 132
BEDFORD, HERBERT, 56
BEETHOVEN, 2, 10 (f.n.), 66, 73, 75 (f.n.), 112–113, 117, 124, 128, 130, 133, 143, 146, 151, 153, 162
BERG, ALBAN, 66, 105, 130, 143, 157, 169–172
BERGFELD, JOACHIM, 116, 137
BERGSON, HENRI, 55
BERLIOZ, 142
Blue Bells of Scotland, 133
Blue Voyage (Riegger), 118, 122
BOSANQUET, BERNARD, 138
BRAHMS, 41, 112, 157
BÜCKEN, ERNST, 28
BUSONI, 68 (f.n.), 83, 135, 157, 161
BUSSLER, LUDWIG, 27 (f.n.)

C

Canon (Hauer), 94–95
CASELLA, ALFREDO, 35, 132
CHANDLER, ALBERT S., 141, 144
CHOPIN, 23, 41, 132
Chromatic Fantasie and Fugue (Bach), 152
Cinq Grimaces (Satie), 117, 119–210
Concerto, for Piano and Orchestra (Delius), 143
Concerto for Orchestra (Piston), 137
CONUS, GEORGE E., 27
COPLAND, AARON, 113, 120, 124–129
COWELL, HENRY, 84 (f.n.)
CZERNY, CARL, 140 (f.n.)

D

DALCROZE, JACQUES, 75–76
DANTE, 159

Dante-Symphony (Liszt), 152
DEBUSSY, 38, 72
DELIUS, FREDERICK, 143
D'INDY, VINCENT, 111–114
Dixie (Emmett), 114
DONOVAN, RICHARD, 56
DUKAS, PAUL, 133

E

ELGAR, EDWARD, 112
EMMANUEL, MAURICE, 75 (f.n.)
Enigma Variations (Elgar), 112
ERPF, HERMANN, 26 (f.n.)
Études Miniatures (Dalcroze), 75–76

F

Fantasie for (Solo) Violin (Hába), 68–70
Fantasie (Hauer), 88, 91–94, 98, 104
Faust-Symphony (Liszt), 152
FECHNER, GUSTAV, 138
Folk-tune (Hungarian), 114
FOULDS, JOHN, 83
FRANCK, CÉSAR, 41, 142–143
French Choral, 21–22
Fünf Geistliche Lieder (von Webern), 51
Für Kinder (Bartók), 66–67
Fugue in C-sharp-minor (Bach), 124
Fugue in B-flat-major (Beethoven, Opus 133), 151

G

GERSHWIN, GEORGE, 76 (f.n.)
GESUALDO, 161
GLYN, MARGARET H., 27 (f.n.)
GOETHE, 159
GOLDSTEIN, WALTER, 66 (f.n.)
Graduale (Eleventh century), 20

H

HÁBA, ALOIS, 19–23, 68–70, 76, 159 (f.n.)
HARBURGER, WALTER, 156
HAUER, JOSEF MATTHIAS, 83–105, 114
Heldenleben, Ein (Strauss, R.), 152
Hin und Zurück (Hindemith), 137
HINDEMITH, PAUL, 36, 53–54, 56, 68 (f.n.), 81 (f.n.), 84 (f.n.), 113, 137, 144, 146–149, 153, 155

177

INDEX

HONEGGER, ARTHUR, 6, 134
HOWELLS, HERBERT, 58

I

If Music be the Food of Love (Bedford), 56
Impromptu, Opus 142 (Schubert), 73

J

JARNACH, PHILLIP, 121
JUHASZ, ANDOR, 148
JUON, PAUL, 143

K

Kammersymphonie (Schoenberg), 109,
144, 171
KELLER, HERMANN, 73
Klavierstücke, Drei, Opus 11 (Schoenberg),
118, 123
Kleine Klavierstücke (Jarnach), 121
KRENEK, ERNST, 38, 139
KURTH, ERNST, 150 (f.n.)

L

LANIER, SIDNEY, 75, 162
LEICHTENTRITT, HUGO, 27 (f.n.)
LISZT, 90, 116, 137, 142, 143 (f.n.), 152
LORENZ, ALFRED, 122, 134, 137, 139, 144
(f.n.)
LOWELL, AMY, 65

M

Ma mère l'oye (Ravel), 9
MACEWEN, J. B., 59 (f.n.)
MACHAULT, GUILLAUME DE, 54
MACPHERSON, STEWART, 16, 27 (f.n.), 73,
133, 145
MAHLER, GUSTAV, 30–31, 34, 128–129,
136
MARENZIO, 161
Meistersinger (Wagner), 152
MILHAUD, DARIUS, 7, 35–36, 152
MOSCHELES, IGNAZ, 133 (f.n.)
MOZART, 2, 9, 11, 28, 31-32, 46

N

NEWMAN, WILLIAM S., 140 (f.n.)
NIETZSCHE, 153
Nocturnes (Debussy), 38

O

OGDEN, R. M., 58
ORNSTEIN, LEO, 5, 24 (f.n.), 78, 132
Overture, Leonore, No. 2 (Beethoven), 75
(f.n.)

P

PALESTRINA, 1–2
PAQUE, DÉSIRÉ, 22
PARRY, C. H., 131
Parsifal (Wagner), 40
PATTERSON, W. M., 65
PFITZNER, HANS, 66
Pieces in the Form of a Pear (Satie), 78
Pierrot Lunaire (Schoenberg), 109
PIJPER, WILLIAM, 142
PISTON, WALTER, 109, 137
Poems (Scott, Cyril), 64–65
Poems of 1917 (Ornstein), 5, 24 (f.n.), 78,
132
Porgy and Bess (Gershwin), 76
POULENC, 137
PRATT, C. C., 55 (f.n.)
Prélude de la Porte Héroique (Satie), 68
Prelude, Interlude and Fugue (Sorabji),
152
Preludes (Chopin), 23, 132
Preludes (Scriabin), 49
Preludes (Shostakovitch), 79
Promenades (Poulenc), 137
Prometheus (Liszt), 152
PROUT, EBENEZER, 27 (f.n.), 32, 46, 50–53,
74, 133

R

RAVEL, MAURICE, 9, 72
REICHENBACH, HERMANN, 55 (f.n.)
RIEGGER, WALLINGFORD, 118, 122
RIEMANN, HUGO, 27 (f.n.), 32–33, 55, 73–
74, 128
Ring des Nibelungen (Wagner), 144 (f.n.)
ROUSSEAU, J. J., 72

S

Sacre du Printemps (Stravinsky), 71
Salome (Strauss, R.), 42
Sancta Johannes (Hymn), 20
SARASATE, PABLO DE, 116
SATIE, ERIK, 68, 78, 117, 119–120
SCHENKER, HEINRICH, 10 (f.n.)
SCHERCHEN, HERMANN, 151 (f.n.)

INDEX

SCHILLINGER, JOSEPH, 83
SCHNABEL, ARTUR, 114–116
SCHOENBERG, ARNOLD, 8, 18–19, 35, 39, 52, 59–60, 71, 83–84, 98, 104–110, 113–114, 116, 118, 123–124, 132, 144, 171–175
SCHOPENHAUER, 41
SCHUBERT, 73, 145–146
SCHUMANN, 41, 66
SCOTT, CYRIL, 64, 159 (f.n.)
SCRIABIN, ALEXANDER, 4, 41–43, 49, 57, 83, 130, 143, 146, 161, 167–169
SEASHORE, CARL, 51 (f.n.)
Sechs Kleine Stücke, Opus 19 (Schoenberg), 116, 118, 123, 132
Sept Pièces brèves (Honegger), 134
SHIELD, WILLIAM, 35 (f.n.)
SHOSTAKOVITCH, DMITRI, 79
SLAVENSKI, JOSEPH, 77
Sonata for Piano (Bartók), 72, 115–117
Sonata for Piano, Opus 2, No. 1 (Beethoven), 133
Sonata for Piano, Opus 2, No. 2 (Beethoven), 133
Sonata for Piano, Opus 10, No. 2 (Beethoven), 133
Sonata for Piano, Opus 49, No. 2 (Beethoven), 133
Sonata for Piano, Opus 26 (Beethoven), 128
Sonata for Piano, Opus 53 (Beethoven), 146
Sonata for Piano, Opus 57 (Beethoven), 133
Sonata for Piano, Opus 101 (Beethoven), 153
Sonata for Piano (Berg), 130, 143
Sonata No. 2 (Busoni), 68 (f.n.)
Sonata for Flute, Viola and Harp (Debussy), 72
Sonata for Flute and Piano (Hindemith), 147
Sonata for Oboe and Piano (Hindemith), 147
Sonata No. 1 for Piano (Hindemith), 144
Sonata No. 3 for Piano (Hindemith), 149, 153
Sonata for (Solo) Viola (Hindemith), 56
Sonata for Viola and Piano, Opus 11, No. 4 (Hindemith), 144, 146
Sonata for Viola and Piano, 1940 (Hindemith), 146

Sonata for (Solo) Violin (Hindemith), 56
Sonata for Violin and Piano, 1935 (Hindemith), 147
Sonata No. 1 for Violin and Piano (Honegger), 6
Sonata for Clarinet and Piano (Juon), 143
Sonata for Piano — 1916 (Milhaud), 7, 36
Sonata for Piano in A-major (Mozart), 28, 46
Sonata for Flute and Piano (Piston), 109 (f.n.)
Sonata for (Solo) Violin (Schnabel), 114, 116
Sonata No. 3 for Piano (Scriabin), 41
Sonata No. 4 for Piano (Scriabin), 41
Sonata No. 5 for Piano (Scriabin), 4, 41, 43–46, 143, 146, 167–169
Sonata No. 6 for Piano (Scriabin), 46
Sonata No. 7 for Piano (Scriabin), 46–48, 57
Sonata for Piano — 1924 (Stravinsky), 137
Sonata No. 2 for Piano (Szymanowski), 130, 155
Sonata No. 3 for Piano (Szymanowski), 130, 155
Sonatina (Busoni), 135
Sonatina (Casella), 132
SORABJI, KAIKHOARU, 152
STEIN, ERWIN, 60, 106 (f.n.), 156, 169, 174
STENGEL, THEOPHIL, 143
STRAUSS, RICHARD, 42, 152–153, 155
STRAVINSKY, IGOR, 11, 71, 137
String Quartet No. 4 (Bartók), 4
String Quartet No. 2 (Hába), 19
String Quartet, Opus 10 (Schoenberg), 109
String Quartet, Opus 56 (Szymanowski) 155
Suite for Piano (Bartók), 36–37
Suite for Piano (Donovan), 56
Suite for Orchestra, Opus 48 (Hauer), 100
Suite, In Green Ways (Howells), 58
Suite, Opus 25 (Schoenberg), 8, 18, 19, 71, 98, 105, 108–109, 113, 118, 172–175
Suites (Krenek), 139
Symphonic Poems (Liszt), 116, 137, 152
Symphonic Poems (Strauss, R.), 152–153, 155
Symphony (Franck), 143
Symphony No. 1 (Mahler), 136
Symphony No. 4 (Mahler), 30–31, 128–129

INDEX

Symphony No. 5, in **B**-flat-major (Schubert), 145–146
SZYMANOWSKI, KAROL, 130, 155

T

Toccata and Chaconne (Krenek), 38
TOVEY, DONALD, 131
Träumerei (Schumann), 66
Trio (Pijper), 142
Trio for Strings (Ravel), 72
Turkish Folk-Song, 21

U

Ungarische Zigeunerweisen (Sarasate), 116

V

Variations for Piano (Copland), 113, 120–129

VANASEK, BENEDICT, 83
VIRUES Y SPINOLA, J. J., 35 (f.n.)

W

WAGNER, V, 3, 9, 32, 39–40, 59, 90, 128, 144 (f.n.)
WEBERN, ANTON VON, 50–53, 57
WHITING, GEORGE, 14 (f.n.)
WIEHMAYER, TH., 75
WILKINSON, C. H., 24
WILLIAMS, ABDY, 27 (f.n.)
Wir bauen eine Stadt (Hindemith), 54
Wozzeck (Berg), 105, 157, 169–172

Z

ZEISING, ADOLF, 138